Only
Just

Jurat Rev. Peter Lane

Copyright © 2024 Jurat Rev. Peter Lane

All rights reserved.

ISBN: 979-8-8842-2596-1

FOR

Wendy,
Julian, Clare and Carys,
Nicolas, Matthew, Georgia, Freya and Robyn,
their offspring and descendants yet unborn
and other close relatives and friends

CONTENTS

	Acknowledgments	i
1	Only Just	1
2	The Crypt School Gloucester	Pg 19
3	Sheffield University	Pg 31
4	Didsbury Methodist Theological College	Pg 41
5	Methodist Circuit Minister	Pg 45
6	The Move to Education	Pg 59
7	Juré Justicier de la Cour Royale	Pg 83
8	Links with Biberach	Pg 101
9	Retirement	Pg 105
10	Credo	Pg 111
11	Sermons on Special Occasions	Pg 125
12	Poetry	Pg 145
13	145 Liminal Limericks	Pg 221
14	Postscript	Pg 254

ACKNOWLEDGMENTS

Wendy who, throughout my Church ministry, teaching career, Jurat service and retirement, and despite her own very onerous life in education, churches and the home, as well as supporting and guiding me with her firm faith and intuitive wisdom, lovingly tolerated my persistent gravitation towards the study and the computer, thus being unreasonably burdened with countless domestic chores associated with housekeeping, cooking, laundering etc., with which I should certainly have been more involved.

Clare, who has shown continuous interest in what I have attempted to write and, with great determination, has found time in her extremely busy and demanding life to acquire the necessary skills to be able to put my jumbled musings into shape for publishing.

Julian, who was Chairman of the *'Guernsey Healing Music Trust'* at the time when Wendy's mother (Nan) was a resident at the Guernsey Residential Home. There I witnessed the remarkable transformation in the residents that was brought about by musicians provided by the Trust.

Georgia, who took us to a demonstration and talk at BAFTA on "Wallace and Gromit" which provided me with the illustration for the sermon I delivered in Gloucester Cathedral.

Graham and Theresa Le Flem, whose warm and close friendship encouraged me to attempt to continue writing poetry, even though my style has always been with rhythm and rhyme, unlike Theresa's, and whose superior technological skills helped Clare to publish 'Only Just'.

ONLY JUST

Chris Claxton, Musician and Composer, the good friend and former colleague who frequently urged me to provide words for him to set to music, resulting in later years in two Good Friday, hour-long Cantatas for St Andrew's Church, Guernsey.

John and Glenys Enticott, who holidayed with us on many occasions, prompting us to visit places which otherwise we would not have seen, thus inspiring me to write *'The Package Holiday'* in Sciathos, and *'Koustoyeriko'*, *'Implicated'* and *'Assumption'* in Crete.

Maureen Pitman who accompanied us to Sri Lanka. She and Wendy persuaded me to stay up all night to witness the walking on fire at *'Kataragama'*.

Keith Langlois, whose exhibition of the war-time tinsel painting of Petit Jacques, for whom he was determined to "right a wrong", prompted me to write *'The S.S.Vega'*.

Sir de Vic Carey, Sir Richard Collas, The Very Rev'd Jeffery Fenwick, Rev Lucy Winket, Rev Brian O'Gorman, Bishop Richard Harries, Rev Graham Haslam, Wolfgang Ottka, The Biberach Friends of Guernsey Committee, Rotraud Rebman, The Old Cryptians Association, Martin Cordall, Rev Alan Ingrouille, Mr R.C.Easterbrook, Warren Barrett, Elaine Storkey, Gitta Sereny, Rabbi Jonathan Sachs, Seamus Heaney, Bernard of Clairvaux.

1 ONLY JUST

Why do we leave it until it is too late before asking our parents and grandparents about their life experiences and childhood memories? If only we had! It is in the expectation that future generations of our family may one day be asking themselves the same question that I am daring to take the presumptuous step of trying to record some of my own memories. May-be by doing this our descendants will be able to place us within the framework of the history of our time.

Why, for example, did I not question my father, Leonard Lane, about his, (as I am told), unexpected survival at birth, his infant frailty, or about his childhood with his three brothers before, during and after the First World War? Or, if only I had asked my mother, she could have identified the songs she had sung on the radio in the 1920's and the circumstances in which she was awarded gold medals for her soprano singing. And is it true that as soon as she married my father, he required her to stop performing on stage? Or was it simply her commitment to the family and particularly to her bed-ridden mother, Lucy Humphris, who had come to live with us before I was born, that caused her to restrict her solo engagements to an occasional song or aria at Church events or at 'Women's Meetings'? And did my father really have to leave school at the outbreak of World War I at the age of 12? Eventually of course he obtained an apprenticeship at Fielding & Platts in Gloucester (where he got the nickname 'Pino', after the singer Pino Lane) and became a skilled carpenter and patternmaker; but that presumably was after his brief military service at the age of 17 in 1919 at Didcot. Only just too young to fight in the First World War, (he was born in 1902 at 22 Regent Street, Gloucester), and too old at 37 years of age to be conscripted for the Second, how fortunate did he feel that he didn't reach 17 until 1919 and thus avoided the carnage of the Somme? Instead, he gained the reputation of being the honest, sober young recruit in the army barracks at Didcot, the non-smoking total abstainer, who could be trusted to look after the other lads' money whilst they went out reveling on Saturday nights.

Dad could turn his hands to most things practical. Soon after his marriage (to my mother Doris Humphris) he, in the 1920's, had set about building in Longford Lane, Gloucester, first a bungalow as their own first home, then a small grocery shop on the corner of Longford Lane and Innsworth Lane in Longlevens, and finally a three-bedroomed semi-detached house, which they named 'Chamwell' in Longford Lane (later to be four bedrooms with the development of the attic as their bedroom to make room for the 'bedridden' Granny Lucy Humphris in theirs), all these properties being within 200 yards of each other. In the 1930's he also set about building a number of static holiday caravans that he sited at Tenby and Weston-super-Mare, but unfortunately both sites were requisitioned for gun sites in 1939 and he lost money when he had to dispose of the caravans very quickly when war broke out. He also spent his spare time making furniture, dining tables, drop-leaf tables and sets of chairs during the '20s and 30s. His motto seemed to be the familiar "The devil finds work for idle hands to do." Indeed, he was always industrious and very serious; but he clearly enjoyed being creative with new wood, especially with oak. At the start of the Second World War he left his three brothers and the family's Chromium-, Nickel -and Silver- Plating Business (which his father and three brothers had established as the Gloucester Plating Company in Victoria Street,) and worked during the day on aircraft propellers at 'Rotol Airscrews' at Staverton airport, followed by further wartime employment in the Gloucester docks; but at night he was often required to be out on A.R.P. (air raid precautions) duties; in spare moments he built a large wooden chicken run and a concrete pigsty, and he produced fruit and vegetables in the garden . Returning to the family plating business when the war ended, he soon found that the fumes from the steaming acid vats affected his breathing. Thus, in 1949 when I was 14, and shortly after the death of Granny Humphris, he bought an 18-acre small holding called 'Twigworth Lawn' in the village of Twigworth on the Gloucester to Tewkesbury Road. There he built more pig sties and pens, converted a barn into cowsheds and kept pigs, geese, chickens and 9 Friesian cows; but later he converted the cowshed into a new home for us, which he called 'Orchard House'; he sold Twigworth Lawn and developed the two old orchards into a very tidy residential park for 100 caravans, mostly 22ft Berkleys, but some Ambassadors which were considerably larger, each with its own fenced garden and pathway. I occasionally was called on to help him break hardcore and unload concrete slabs for the roads and pathways he constructed and hold tools for him as he built shower rooms, laundry rooms, a telephone box and a little shop for the caravan residents, which he stocked, and my mother ran. I also helped sometimes with delivering milk and collecting the 10 shillings a week ground rent from each caravan owner. I learnt to drive when I was 16 to enable me to tow around the caravan sites the home-made cesspit tank, which helped him considerably with the necessary but unpleasant task of emptying the 100 *Elsan* toilets twice a week. There is no doubting that he worked extremely hard, and valued his tools so highly that I was never allowed to use them. He was completely lost if ever one was not in its correct slot, but he ensured that they were never allowed to rest for long in their allotted places.

The Redundant Tool-Shed

My father, being a trained carpenter/patternmaker, treasured his tools to such an extent that I was expected never to touch them, apart from to pass them to him as he was working. He worked extremely hard and hoped that by studying I would have "an easier life". He died in Church on 11th October 1974, aged 72, of a heart attack whilst trying to lift a piano off the carpet that he was mending (as his father had done when lifting a sack of coal in the cellar at 22 Regent Street). On the day of his funeral, I stepped inside his toolshed and simply stood and stared in amazement. I was being 'watched'.

Spirit levels quivered, nerves they tried to hide
Pincers grew attentive too. Pliers stood astride.
Planes awoke for shaving. Saws showed polished teeth.
Vices, benched, with jaws unclenched. Knives in every sheath.
Well rehearsed for action, wedges in their sets;
Mallets planned percussion and drills their pirouettes.
Chisels by the dozen, sharp, with gleaming blade.
Bradawls stood, as soldiers should, upright on parade.
Files were rough and ready, brace with bits aflirt,

ONLY JUST

> Two-foot rules and other tools loth to be inert,
> Nails and screws contended, vying for their turn,
> Not a care and unaware what they were to learn.
> Each turned round bewildered, sensed perhaps a catch,
> Shocked to see that it was me fumbling at the latch.
> "Henceforth you're redundant," grievingly I said,
> "Your platoon will split up soon. The carpenter is dead.
> Could I but be your master, I'd join your fun and games;
> But father led me from your shed. To me you're simply names."

P.G.L.

In any case, his hope for us three children was that we might grow up to use our brains and therefore "not have to work so hard". But if only I had asked more questions, I might have acquired some of his practical skills, as did my brother Sebert (whose skills came, I believe, more through the genes and perseverance than by father's instruction). With so little education and being born at the cross-over between Victoria's reign and Edwardian times in 1902, father unfortunately had little education, a rather narrow, prudish approach to life and an unquestioning, literalist approach to the Bible. He was deeply committed to his faith and to Methodism, and to total abstinence in particular. He never smoked, apart from one day every year. We knew it was Christmas by the welcome smell of the Manikin Cigar that pervaded the house only on that day. Christmas 1946 sticks in my memory particularly because, having hoped to receive may-be a football, their present to me at the age of 11 consisted of a small, black leather-bound Authorised Version of the Bible, which didn't go down too well; it certainly wasn't written for children of 11, but I probably had to try hard to hide my disappointment.

Having been brought up at Ryecroft Methodist Sunday School close to his Regent Street Home, he had been a member of the tea-total 'Band of Hope' as well as of the Victorian 'Rechabites' (based on Jeremiah chapter 35) and sang tenor in the Church Choir. But with the arrival of children Dad and Mum (who had been brought up at Brunswick Road Baptist Church) moved to worship at Lonsdale Road Methodist Church, where he taught in the Sunday School, and also throughout WW2 ran the Tuesday night Junior Guild. On the one hand he could be impetuously generous and hard-working, and on the other, puritanical, quite dogmatic and, in the home, intolerant of opinions other than his own. As the youngest, I soon learnt, by observing what happened with my sister Grace (seven years older than me) and my brother Sebert (my senior by four years), that it was safest never to question or discuss things in general and things religious in particular, and certainly never to voice an opinion. In fact, seldom to open my mouth. My thoughts therefore remained my own. The absence of any open discussion within the family resulted in my feeling somewhat inferior to other lads who could voice their views and opinions clearly and forcibly.

I had witnessed the heated rows brought on when Grace and Sebert dared to express the more enlightened, liberal thoughts that they had picked up at school. So I remained silent, and as a youngster I engrossed myself in hobbies, - collecting foreign stamps, foreign coins, train numbers, collecting autographs and (to my later shame) birds' eggs; I fingered out on the piano lots of tunes from the Methodist hymn book and escaped the home as much as possible, to hit a tennis ball, kick a football or to roller-skate the one mile along the Longford Lane, which was totally devoid of traffic in war-time. Sadly, although I was taught to read at an early age by my sister, using antiquated booklets, there were no children's books of any interest at home apart from the heavy volumes of Arthur Mee's 'Children's Encyclopedia', so I never came to enjoy reading. Nonetheless, strangely, I was frequently chosen to be the one to read in public at Lonsdale Road Sunday School and later at the Crypt School where I became a pupil at the age of eight (when it was still an independent direct-grant school). In fact, I won prizes at School as a Prefect, as well as later at Theological College for elocution and for reading in public. Grace also encouraged me to sing treble solos, so that I became somewhat in demand for singing such as "Who is Sylvia?", "The soldiers of the King" and other songs at Church social events. In my teens, table tennis and tennis at the Lonsdale Road Methodist Youth Club occupied several evenings a week in winter and summer, with mixed hockey for Wesley Hall Youth Club at weekends. Our Youth Club leader was Bill Hook who played rugby at fullback for Gloucester and, for two seasons, for England. He entered our Youth Club in one of the Gloucester Table Tennis Leagues, and surprisingly we didn't lose all our matches. We held him in high esteem, so languid did he appear on the rugby field, but he was always in the right place, and was so accurate with his kicking, and of course could beat us all at table-tennis.

Money during the war had been quite scarce in our family. My mother budgeted with great care, and she managed to feed us on the very meager rations allowed during the war, but with the help of our own eggs (often preserved in 'water-glass') and occasionally our own pork or rabbit. I had inherited toys which my father had made for my brother and sister, such as wooden stilts at which I became very proficient, and a damaged four wheeled go-cart propelled by pulling hard on a central lever and guided by one's feet. When Sebert and I yearned for a cricket bat dad managed to persuade his eldest brother, my Uncle Chris who had no children, to buy us a secondhand cricket bat, which turned out to be far too heavy for me to use. I received a small amount of pocket money (2 or 3 pence per week), which he occasionally supplemented with a boost if we succeeded in learning, at his suggestion, the words of a hymn off by heart or the list of all the books of the Bible in sequence, both Old and New Testaments. Little did I realize at the time just how useful the latter would prove to be in later life. Nor did I appreciate until much later in life what a fortunate, safe, sober, secure upbringing I experienced in time of war when many of my friends' fathers were away in the forces, some never to return. Parents had much to worry about, worries from which we three children were mercifully sheltered; but life at home was rather stern and serious.

I would often escape with my friends to play football or to do my own private scorekeeping at the local cricket ground. RAF Innsworth was also only a mile away, and every evening and at week- ends there was a constant stream of mostly Canadian, but occasionally Australian airmen walking to town, passing the Longlevens cross-roads close to home. I was quite successful at a form of polite begging, relieving them of foreign stamps from their letters, foreign coins, chewing gum and very occasionally cigarettes. And when no cigarettes came my way, it was not unknown for me and my friends to try smoking little dry tubular honeysuckle stems, or even to unpack dog-ends that the airmen had dropped and roll my own with the contents. Father was too busy in the 1940's to find out, what with his work, his wartime ARP duties, running the Junior Guild at Church, teaching in the Sunday School and doing home improvements, fitting a central heating system throughout the house and building war-time concrete pig sties and a large underground air raid shelter in the garden at Chamwell, Longford Lane. We all retreated to or were carried whilst asleep to the shelter during the war on any night when the sirens sounded, denoting enemy aircraft approaching. They were heading mostly for Coventry, but occasionally dropped any left-over bombs close by on their return journey. Our hope was to find maybe a few pieces of shrapnel on the way to school. They were regarded as trophies worth collecting or valuable for exchanging.

Sunday Schools thrived during the war. It was somewhere for children to go on Sunday afternoons and the teachers were deeply committed and caring. Lonsdale Road Sunday School had five Departments, each with several classes of around half a dozen children. Looking back one can recall singing hymns such as "Marching beneath the banner, Fighting beneath the cross", "We've a story to tell to the nations that will set my people free", "Onward, Christian soldiers, marching as to war" or "Remember all the people who live in far-off lands…. where apes swing to and fro," which we sang heartily but now sound hideously militaristic, imperialist and 'woke'. Each week we would hear read out the names of former pupils who were either "Killed in action", "Missing, presumed dead", "Prisoner of war", or simply "Reported missing". It was all very gloomy, as were the Church services. That is, until V.E. Day on May 8th, 1945, when suddenly, instead of singing regularly "O valiant hearts, who to your glory came," we sang with verve and tremendous gusto "Mine eyes have seen the glory of the coming of the Lord". It was new to me at the age of 10, and I remember vividly singing it loudly and heartily all the way home and dancing as I sang it repeatedly on top of the air-raid shelter halfway down the garden as my mother finished cooking the Sunday roast.

One weekly task I undertook was to take home every Sunday the two name-boards from the frame outside Church. These announced the identity of the two preachers planned to lead the worship on the following Sunday. I had a reputation for having very tidy handwriting and I knew I could make a better job of signwriting in white chalk the preachers' names than the person who simply scribbled them. So, I studied Roman script and carefully worked on the names each week, making certain to include any titles or degrees they had. Unconsciously I must have been cementing in my mind at that young age the significance of having titles and letters after one's name. Despite my lack of enthusiasm for reading, studying and learning, it gradually became something of a subconscious ambition one day perhaps to acquire some letters after my name. Perhaps it is partly this which contributed to my becoming the first member of our family ever to go to university.

Yet my hardworking father, serious and narrow-minded as he was, strict non-smoker, tea-totaller and firm observer of the Sabbath (Sunday), had a kind heart and was well meaning. By 1946 the Airforce men at RAF Innsworth and at Elmbridge had been replaced by German Prisoners of War. In 1947 the prisoners from the nearby P.O.W. camp at Elmbridge were allowed out for a few hours on Sunday evenings, to go for a walk or to attend Church. By the age of twelve I was old enough to attend Church with the whole family three times every Sunday. I would invent any excuse (usually gastric) to miss the morning service because of a certain Mr. Humphries (no relation) who often writhed uncontrollably on the floor, having terrifying screaming fits which, I was told, resulted from his having been gassed in the First World War.

Less terrifying, but nonetheless the cause at first of

considerable anxiety when I was twelve, was the large gathering of German POWs in their rough, patched uniforms who filled our Church at evening services with their powerful singing and strange language. Throughout the war I had never felt in any way insecure or threatened. Parents somehow succeeded in reassuring their children that there was nothing to fear. Dad had even told me that he didn't believe God would ever allow Hitler to win the war. I remember precisely where we were walking in the Innsworth Lane when he shared this particular thought with me, thinking presumably that I may have been living in some fear; but I certainly never did.

In 1942 when I was seven, I had spent many long weeks in bed with scarlet fever and acute nephritis, which I 'only just' managed to survive. There were no antibiotics available to the general public. Penicillin had been discovered, but it was only available for members of His Majesty's armed forces. The only drug prescribed for me had been M & B tablets, which gave me horrendous hallucinations. At the age of 88, as I write, I can still visualize them vividly. I can still clearly visualize the aircraft landing and taking off on my bedroom curtains that stretched to the bottom of our long garden, and seeing not one but three boiled eggs on my breakfast plate as I sat up in bed. Years later Sebert explained how he had seen my mother crying in the kitchen, thinking I was not likely to survive. My temperature was constantly around 105 degrees Fahrenheit, and by the age of eight I was down to three stone seven. I certainly missed a lot of schooling at Longlevens Junior School. Five years later I contracted nephritis again but recovered more quickly, probably because penicillin by then had become available to the general public. Perhaps it was for these reasons, as well as the fact that I was a very fussy eater, that I was, and have always remained, underweight, if not skeletal.

I had used soap to stick dozens of photographs to my bedroom walls, all cut from the Gloucester 'Citizen'. They were head and shoulder pictures of our local lads who had been killed or reported missing. Some had been members of our Church. Now, in 1947 when I was 12, the rows of seats on Sunday evenings were filled with huge, strong men more than three times my size. These were "the enemy." So, I wondered subconsciously, 'what if they suddenly turned on us?' Nonetheless that was nothing like the terror that gripped me on Sunday mornings, when I hoped and prayed that my home-spun superstitious mantras might possibly prevent the uncontrollable writhing, the foaming at the mouth and the screeching of the WW1 veteran and victim of the gas attacks, Mr. Humphries.

Soon, with a wonderful lesson in forgiveness and reconciliation, encouraged, I suspect, by the Minister, my parents started inviting a group of Prisoners of War, the biggest men I had ever encountered, to our home for afternoon tea before the Sunday evening Service. This was so unusual, for we never had visitors to tea, unless it was a long-planned visit from an aunt or great uncle paying a visit to see their bed-ridden mother (or cousin). Occasional acts of charity, particularly in bitterly cold weather, would mean a group of gypsies selling pegs might be found in the front room drinking a cup of tea and warming themselves, and I would be asked to sit with them to make sure nothing 'disappeared'. This happened particularly in the 'deep freeze' winter of 1946/47, when snow lay over 6 feet deep for weeks on end and narrow walkways were dug the length of our road with very high walls of snow on either side. When the thaw eventually came Gloucester became flooded; we couldn't get to school at the Crypt, and two cousins living at Minsterworth who got to school in town ended up having to stay at our house. 'Sleepovers' had never been heard of, so it was a most unusual event. And when the flooded fields froze, we enjoyed skating and sliding the length of the local playing fields. Members of the armed forces who turned up at Church might also be invited home for lunch, several on a more regular basis. My cousin Humphrey Wall, in the RAF, actually brought his wife and baby, Michael, to lodge with us for several months whilst he was stationed at RAF Innsworth. Quite a demanding experience.

For the German POWs It was usually Scotch pancakes smeared with a hint of margarine (since our butter ration was so minute), together with genteel cups of tea, that my mother prepared for them on Sunday afternoons. It all looked so incongruous in their enormous hands. One of them, who wore size 13 in boots, had the surname Luther and came from Wittenberg (which by then was in the Russian Zone). Yes, Reinhold Luther. He explained that he was a descendent of the great 16th century Protestant Reformer Martin Luther. It meant nothing to me at the time, but I still treasure his autograph and the photograph I took of him and my father, together in our garden. I was using the box camera that once belonged to my late Uncle Sebert (the much adored and only brother of my mother). It was such experiences that caused me a year later, when it came to choosing between Arts or Science at school, to opt for the Arts, because by that route I could learn German. This turned out to be quite a major yet unwitting turning point in my life, for German was something I would eventually greatly enjoy teaching and Germany a country I would love visiting. But why did my father so firmly think that the louder he shouted, the more likely it would be that the POWs would understand his

English? I never dared ask. Most Sundays the Germans brought us gifts they had made during the week. Several times they brought us slippers made out of coarse binder twine, - a pair for each member of the family. When eventually they left us, they promised to write, but we suspect that they probably never reached their homes, for we never heard from any of them again. If only we had made more inquiries at that time. Almost 70 years late, in retirement, prior to visiting Wittenberg as part of a cruise down the river Elbe we attempted to trace any relatives of Reinhold Luther, but without success. We discovered that there were no surviving direct relatives of the great Reformer, but it was suggested that Reinhold could have been a descendent of one of Martin Luther's brothers. Like many other former P-O-W's due to return to the Russian zone in Germany they may well have been sent to Siberia, so we were told.

If only I had put more questions to my mother about the circumstances of her only brother's death. My Uncle Sebert was a Corporal killed in "No-man's-land" beyond the trenches on 31st March 1918. In the 2nd/5th Battalion Gloucestershire Regiment and the Royal Corps of Signals, he was awarded the Military Medal posthumously for trying to repair telephone wires in 'no-man's-land'. Around 1990 Wendy and I took flowers and found his grave among the well-kept, tidy ranks of headstones in a small British war cemetery at Holnon in Northern France (Plot 1, Row F, Grave 14). Only my sister (with her husband Peter Hillier) and Wendy and I had ventured there to show our respect in almost 100 years; but sadly, between their visit and ours someone had stolen the Book of Remembrance in which Grace had written her tribute. Presumably the news of his death reached his parents and four sisters on a Sunday. It usually did. But what effect did it have on the family?

Certainly, my mother grieved for many years the loss of her elder brother whom she had idolized and adored. And what happened to the poetry he had written? I recall as a child reading his simple, jingoistic poems in pamphlets of the Gloucestershire Regiment strangely entitled "The Gurkha". If only I had asked more questions! On the centenary of Uncle Sebert's death in 2018 Wendy and I, accompanied by my brother-in-law Peter Hillier, visited the war memorial in Gloucester Park to lay flowers beneath his name, which appears erroneously in two different places at the site (one of them mistakenly spelled adding an 'e' to the name Humphris before the last letter).

I wonder why my father destroyed almost all memories of him the moment my grandmother died, including his wonderful collection of glass slides depicting his colleagues at war, and his poems? Did he think it might help my mother to stop grieving and bring closure? My granny had lived with us for the first 13 years of my life, she had been bed-ridden for as long as I could remember, and my mother looked after her. All tribute to them for willingly taking her into their care in their home, for such kindness and willingness is far less possible and less common as I write in 2023. I used to take up her meals, collect her dishes, eat up her apple and pear peelings and, daily, thread her needles. She spent her days knitting 'squares' to make blankets and tea-cozies. She had given me Uncle Sebert's box-camera (that unfortunately let in the light), and his collection of match-box labels and foreign coins, when I was twelve. My sister Grace inherited his war medals, but what happened to all the sepia glass-plate photographs of him and his colleagues in their military uniforms, the fading copies of the "Gurkha" and other memorabilia when Granny died? They must have been destroyed in our move, in 1949, to the small holding

ONLY JUST

(Twigworth Lawn), two miles outside Gloucester on the Tewkesbury Road, and the resulting changes in my parents' lives that became possible the moment she died. She had been born in 1856, just at the end of the Crimean war. If only I had asked her about her memories of Queen Victoria, of the Empire and the Boer War, about the first local DCL Yeast Company that her husband William had established in Longsmith Street in Gloucester, and especially about the fact that she had given birth to my mother, by far the youngest of her 5 children, at the ripe age of 46. Such things were just not questioned in those days. But at that rather advanced age, to find oneself expecting a child would surely have been surprising, to say the least, if not considered an unintended accident.

If only I had asked my paternal grandfather Raymond Lane about the founding of his Gloucester Plating Company in Victoria Street, in which all four of his sons worked until my father left on health grounds or enquired as to how he had taught himself to play the banjo. Had he ever suspected that the chopped-up cabbage that he readily ate and enjoyed was in fact the Brussels sprouts he claimed he so hated, or that Granny Lane had always insisted my father, as a child, should water down the beer he was regularly sent to fetch for him from the pub at the end of Regent Street. What was the unique variety of apples, so loved by the flying insects and grubs, that fell from the tree that leant over the greenhouse and fishpond at 22 Regent Street? They had a delicious, scented flavour, one I would always recognize but sadly have never found in any other apple since? And why did Granny Lane always give me a present each time I visited after my Saturday morning piano lesson - usually a gift brought to her by some recent visitor? And why did she call the goldfish 'Jasper Phelps' and serenade it melodiously with an old song

"Beyond those Jasper walls"?

Why did I never ask Granny Lane (nee Pollard) about her father William Pollard (1833-1909)? He had moved from Burnley in Lancashire and became one of the pioneers of the Cooperative Movement in Gloucester. He was elected as the first President of the Gloucester Cooperative and Industrial Society Ltd at its inaugural meeting held in the Hope Inn, Barton Street on July 17th, 1860. But there would have been so much more she could have told us.

What, if anything, had my paternal grandfather Raymond Lane (Granny Lane's husband) heard from *his* mother or his maternal grandfather? Did he (my great-great grandfather) ever tell him about the dreadful accident on the River Severn on 24th February, 1835? Morrison Hodges (my Grandpa Raymond Lane's grandfather) was apparently only 22 and was already Master of a canal boat. According to the newspaper report he was being towed up-river just outside Gloucester on a very windy day when the river was in flood. The boat was being towed by the Steamer *Sabrina*. She steered to avoid a barge going down the river. The canal boat floundered and took in water. Being heavily laden with pig iron she tipped and sank in deep water. Morrison's young wife Mary, together with two of their daughters, Maria and Sarah, were in the cabin. Unable to get out, all three were drowned. The coroner recorded it as 'Accidental death'. It was also mentioned that had it not been for the heroic efforts of the crew of the steamer, the lives of Morrison Hodges (the Master), a child of about 3 years of age and another man would also have been lost.

If Morrison had not been rescued, or if Mary had not tragically drowned, he would never have taken Ann Jones as his second wife. Then the daughter of that union would of course never have been born in 1852. Neither would my grandfather Raymond Lane in 1876, nor consequently my father Leonard in 1902. And so on. Did they know anything of this? And what countless quirks of fate result in any of us being here today? Or is there not more to it than that? Did we *only just* make it, or are we each, as the founder of Methodism regarded himself as being "A *brand plucked from the burning",* saved for a purpose ?

.

2 THE CRYPT SCHOOL, GLOUCESTER (1943-54)
A CLOSE-RUN THING

1942 was the year in which I missed quite a lot of schooling through illness. It was also the year in which my elder brother Sebert (so named after his late Uncle) started as an 11-year-old fee-payer at the independent (as it was then) Crypt School. The following year saw the publication of a Government White Paper on the future of Education; this was to lead to the famous 1944 Education Act. It suggested a tripartite system of Grammar, Technical and Secondary Modern Schools, all funded by the State. This would enable all pupils to have the sort of education for which they were apparently considered best suited, free of charge, with the minimum school leaving age rising to 15. Free transport and free milk would also be provided for all pupils. The Directors of the Crypt decided that, with the City Council's support, the school should cease to be an independent direct-grant school and become a State-run Grammar School.

A new building for the Crypt School had been started before

the war at Podsmead. Although unfinished, it was decided nonetheless to open it in September 1943. In order that I might be in the right place for the moment when RAB Butler's 1944 Education Act came into force, and in the hope that I might be helped to catch up on the education I had missed through so much illness, my parents decided to start paying for me to attend the Crypt Junior Department, knowing that when the Bill became law in 1944 my education in the Junior Department would be free of charge from then on, and might be able to continue into the Grammar School at 11. Another reason for sending me there was probably the fact that the Form Teacher of 1B (the class for 8-year-olds) was Harry Dawes, who had been with my father in the Army at Didcot in 1919. Thus from 1944 my education cost my parents nothing and I was in the right place to take the 11+ exam with good prospects of success (known as the 'scholarship') and of remaining at the Crypt in 1946. Although Longlevens was only 2 miles from the city centre and 4 miles from the new school building, we were outside the city boundary. It was thus that the future of only 2 boys in my class was decided at the Shire Hall, I being one of them. I sat the 'County' Scholarship exams in the William Tyndale Hall, and we were tested in Arithmetic and English. In addition, I had to undergo an interview in the Shire Hall, at which I recall being questioned on *The Wind in the Willows,* which we had been reading in school.

The fact that my parents had taken this initiative in 1943 meant that three years later, at 11, I found myself in the fast four-year "A" stream of a Grammar School oriented towards academic achievement, - a school of which I was to be a pupil for no less than 11 years. Having said that, the world of school and life at home were light years apart. They bore no relation to each other. Parents' Evenings were unheard of.

Parents were kept at a distance and in ignorance of pupils' progress, except for the annual school report which, more often than not, merely indicated 'fair', 'satisfactory' or 'unsatisfactory'. No-one at home was ever able to help me with schoolwork, nor did I want them to, for I was afraid of revealing my ignorance. My sister by this time had gone off to Southlands Methodist Teacher Training College in Wimbledon. Nor did I want my parents to help me. Conversation never revolved around things academic, cultural or political, not mathematical, historical, geographical, scientific or linguistic, as they did at the home of my cousins, Janet, Patsy and Susan, who lived out at Minsterworth who called themselves 'Appethonians', after the name of their house 'Appethorn'. There, apparently, they had regular family quizzes at mealtimes and discussions of the studies being pursued; they went to concerts and plays. My sister, being 7 years older, had left home for college when I was 11. My brother was 4 years ahead of me, and on the five-year course, for he was in the B stream; and like me, I guess, he was struggling somewhat. I was therefore simply expected to take care of my own schoolwork. A further spell of nephritis at the age of 13, combined with the fact that I was the youngest (born in July) and smallest in my form, meant that I got further and further behind in class. I was extremely reluctant to reveal my ignorance by asking questions and hoped I would never be asked one. I hid my lack of understanding and the onset of puberty behind plenty of silly behaviour, and this resulted in my father being summoned to the school one day to discuss the matter. This was virtually unheard of. It must have been a huge ordeal for him, for although he was a jack of all trades in things practical, my mother, a shorthand typist, was mathematically and linguistically the brighter of the two and it was she who handled financial matters. Was I to remain at the school or be put into the B or C stream? It was possibly a close-run thing. However, it was decided that I would remain in the A stream (because they seemed to think I was fairly intelligent) but should stay down a year; thus it would take me 5 years (instead of the usual "A stream" 4 years) to journey from 11+ to 'O' levels, just as it was for all boys in the B and C streams, such as my brother. It proved to be a successful move, for instead of always being at the bottom of the class in most subjects, I now ended up very near the top. This, together later with my remaining in the sixth form for 3 years meant I was a pupil at the Crypt continuously from 1943 to 1954, probably longer than any boy before or since, and I eventually scraped into university, - but only just.

Despite a change of Headmaster when D. G. Williams retired, his successor Colin Ewan continued the same format for the daily School Assembly. A hymn was always followed by a Bible Reading, read by a rota of Prefects, and the one and only prayer recited repeatedly by the Head, "......... who has safely brought us to the beginning of this day, defend us in the same with thy mighty power and grant that this day we fall into no sin, neither run into any kind of danger; but that all our doings may be ordered by thy governance, to do always that is righteous......" etc.

In Harry Dawes's School Choir during those years, I progressed from Treble (head chorister) through to Alto, Bass and finally Tenor. *'Lead me, Lord,' 'Non nobis, domine,' 'Let the bright seraphim,' and 'In sanae et vanae curae'* were frequently sung, together with countless other anthems and many a Psalm, and certain major school events, such as Founders' Days and Carol Services, were held in Gloucester Cathedral, with Herbert Sumpsion at the organ. The Queen's

Coronation in 1953 was celebrated in the City Park by a combined schools performance of *Merrie England*. But I remained linked with Methodism because my father declined the invitation from Harry Dawes for me to join his excellent Church choir at an Anglican Church in Westgate Street, where he was organist and choir master.

School meals were, like Latin, something to be dreaded. Latin, because the Master, Moggy Brown seemed determined to humiliate and terrify boys into absorbing every bit of grammar and vocabulary, and mocked those who couldn't grasp it first time. It was the use of his eyes and his sarcasm, together with the vicious use of his hands that we feared. Like many of the older Masters, he had fought in the First World War, and his methods perhaps reflected what he had been through. School dinners were also dreaded. Admittedly a very fussy eater, I found them unappetizing and, if Harry Dawes or Moggy Brown was on duty, mealtimes were occasions for retching. These two, because of food shortages, and reminding us of 'the starving millions', insisted that every plate was to be empty before they were cleared away. Thus, one hesitant shirker could hold up the rest and reduce the time for 'weak horses', playground football or other pursuits in the playground. The puddings were the worst. If it was not the semolina, it was the sago or the tapioca that I found simply impossible to swallow. Nor would it, unlike the sickly spam and putrid potato, go in my pocket. So, I soon learnt to break school rules and escape from the grounds at lunchtimes. In my early days at the Crypt my meals had cost only 3d a day. The oldest child (my sister Grace) paid 5d, the next (Sebert) 4d, and the third 3d. Three "old" pence was scarcely enough to buy a bag of chips, and so I survived on may-be a dripping cake or the scratching's left over when the fish came out of the fat at the chip shop. Anything was better than being compelled to eat the revolting food from the school canteen. The fact that I was never caught for leaving the premises was also a close-run thing, but by an early age I had acquired from home some of the skills required in the art of avoiding detection. The consequences could have been serious had I been caught.

At 'O' level I obtained good passes in English Language, English Literature, Maths, History, French and German, but failed Physics most miserably. Latin required a second attempt before I eventually scraped through. My behaviour must have improved, for I was eventually made a prefect, and since, like my father, I could apparently be trusted with money, I was put in charge of the school tuck shop for my final two years. We sold around 300 doughnuts every morning during the 15-minute break-time and, at lunchtimes, when it became more available and off rations after the war, a lot of chocolate and fizzy drinks after school dinners.

At home it was important always to give the impression of being busy, otherwise jobs, usually of a heavy, labouring nature, helping my father, would be found. "The devil finds work for idle hands to do" was quoted time and time again. Such tasks might vary from cracking rocks for roadbuilding on the caravan site, to unloading concrete slabs, climbing very high ladders to pick fruit, or simply to passing prescribed tools to my father as he called for them. I didn't mind helping; it was the prospect of receiving impromptu home-spun sermons I didn't enjoy. Helping father might involve driving the car (at a young age) around the residential site that he had established at Twigworth Lawn, whilst he emptied the 100 'Elsan' toilet buckets into his brilliantly constructed home-made trailer-tank. It never included being present when a cow was calving or a sow was delivering her litter, for such experiences were regarded as prurient, since they verged on matters sexual, which I was thereby influenced to believe, rather than being something truly and divinely wonderful, had something to do with sordidness and sin. Whatever it was, one could expect it to be accompanied by some moralizing and thus to be avoided if possible. Not that all his ideas were misguided; it was usually the sternness with which they were delivered that I wanted to escape. There was not much fun. It was clear that, like the milk we delivered with a ladle from churn to jug (and later by bottle), and just as the cream always rose to the top, he wanted to encourage me always to (as he put it) "aim to be the cream." It accorded with the parable of the talents and could be summed up in a motto learnt at a Junior Guild meeting, - 'Beyond the best there is a better'. This was nothing to do with money, but everything to do with Christian virtue, character and vocation.

This did not help a great deal with my academic work. It did, however, encourage me, if I had no homework, to be out of the house whenever possible, and eventually to want to travel. When at home, apart from schoolwork I/we never read anything other than the occasional News Chronicle or the daily Gloucester 'Citizen'. We had no television until I was 18, and then it was only a tiny screen relaying one black and white channel with one programme, the BBC, and that was domestically monitored and strictly censored. I had watched the Coronation of the Queen in 1953 on a tiny television set at the home of Grace's boyfriend, Peter Hillier. Since there was very little conversation at our home, I spent hours learning to play most of the tunes in the Methodist hymn book, having abandoned piano lessons at grade 3 or 4 when I was about 10 because the teacher used a ruler on my fingers when I got the fingering wrong when playing scales. My learning to play hymn tunes meant that on Sunday evenings after Church I could occasionally accompany the hymn singing at the home of the wonderful Mr and Mrs Buttling, who held what they called "A Squash" for young people. About 15-25 of us teenagers used to crowd into their lounge, eat biscuits, drink tea, sing hymns in four-part harmony and hold discussions. It was there that for the first time we heard the sound of our own voices, for Mr. B borrowed a tape-recorder from his work. That 'Squash' was influential on many young people's lives, producing three Methodist Ministers and numerous church leaders of the future. Leslie Buttling was a lecturer in the Commerce Department at the local College of F.E. and a Local Preacher, and his wife always seemed to have an open home, welcoming us to meals and gladly buying off me the fresh eggs my own chickens had laid.

Holidays during the war were out of the question. My earliest memory was in the Summer of 1939 staying at Penelly, just outside Tenby in one of the caravans Dad had built. They were not for towing but had two small black metal wheels. I recall that to get to the beach we had to walk across a railway line and sand dunes. In 1945 or '46 we went and stayed with Mum's sister, Aunty Nellie and her husband, the rather strict and serious Rev Frank Savage. He was Baptist Minister in Naunton, in the Cotswolds. He insisted on every plate being empty at the end of every meal. This I dreaded, so I was glad in the following years that they went away when we arrived and left us to it. As I was the youngest, we went to Naunton without Grace and Sebert. There was nothing to do apart from taking daily walks with my parents, which they seemed to enjoy, but I certainly didn't. Eventually at the age of 12 or 13 I persuaded them to let me catch a bus into Cheltenham each day, to get to the annual County Cricket Festival, where I kept my own score-book of every ball bowled and ate the soggy tomato sandwiches my mother had packed for my lunch. My Uncle and Aunt had seven grown-up children, who by this time had left home, and several were still in the Forces. Later, two were ordained into the priesthood of the Anglican Church (Humphrey and David Savage).

One of Uncle Frank and Aunty Nellie's children, Betty, had married a farm bailiff, Leon Budden. They lived in Shaftesbury, Dorset, and later at Box, near Bath. As soon as I was sixteen, I bought a second-hand Francis Barnet 98cc autocycle with the £20 my Grandpa Lane had left for each of his grandchildren in his will. I used it to get to school. But in the Summer holidays I rode it to their farm, spending days stooking up wheat sheaves or sitting beside Leon on the tractor as he cut the wheat using the binder. As the binder approached the centre of a vast field, the rabbits would be seen scampering in all directions. I would leap off the tractor in pursuit and dispatch several each day rather cruelly, some of which were sold or given away; others were skinned, drawn and cooked for next day's evening meal. I have always had rather an ambivalent relationship with rabbits, for as a young child I not only kept pet mice, but also rabbits that I adored and bred. Sometimes, when they got too numerous, and my father would allegedly 'sell' one or two and give me an extra three-penny bit as pocket money. Unbeknown to me at the time, the so-called 'chicken' we occasionally ate for lunch on the Sunday was not chicken at all, but rabbit.

The idea of travelling abroad was suggested by my Form Teacher, Mr. Easterbrook, to whose encouragement I owe a great deal. He was one of the younger members of Staff recently returned from the Second World War, an inspirational teacher of German and French. He believed that learning German in particular could promote understanding and reconciliation. His organized trips were too expensive for our family to afford, and in any case my brother had already had his, and the family's fingers, burnt by a trip organizer who had run off with everyone's money. So, when the school received a letter from a lad in Ratingen, Düsseldorf, wanting a penfriend and a possible exchange, I jumped at the idea. I was 17 and it was Easter-time in 1952. Hitch-hiking down the Autobahn from Düsseldorf, via Cologne, Bonn, Frankfurt, Würzburg, Ulm, Nuremberg and Bamberg to the Bodensee (Lake Constance) and back, often in driving rain and with inadequate clothing, was no fun, neither was sleeping rough in barns and the occasional Youth Hostel. The two of us lived on hard boiled eggs, and very coarse bread, spread with margarine and German 'Schmierwurst', apart from the occasional very basic Youth Hostel meal. Wolfgang Ottka and I never hit it off, but it certainly gave a boost to my conversational German. Having already passed seven 'O' levels (English Lang., English Lit., Maths, History, German and French, and at second attempt, Latin), and having soon dropped History as an A level subject, I had proceeded with just German and French (but both also at scholarship level) as my two A level subjects.

One of the places we visited on our hitch-hiking expedition was the small medieval town of Rothenburg-ob-der-Tauber. It was and still is surrounded by its ancient medieval wall. It happened to be Good Friday, and I felt it right to visit the Church. I was soon ushered out, and it wasn't surprising. Having slept rough, wearing borrowed clothing and with a huge Rucksack made me very conspicuous as worshippers gathered. Somewhat disappointed, I climbed up into the town wall where my eyes were immediately attracted by the sight of a small hill outside the town, on which stood just three trees. For me, mysteriously, they became three Crosses, and they have had a lasting impression on me to this day. Something clicked within me, and it is clear that some bells must have rung, or voice must have spoken as I stood there, - a voice that recurred in the following years when singing hymns, hearing moving sermons and meeting remarkable people of faith.

From a very young age I had heard stories of heroes of the Christian faith who achieved great things in their lives. They were people with a purpose. One in particular was of course John Wesley who was rescued from his father's rectory at Epworth in Lincolnshire, when the house was on fire. From that moment onwards he regarded himself as the 'brand plucked from the burning' and plucked for a specific vocation; and he used that phrase as a euphemism in his preaching, referring to all Methodists as 'brands plucked from the eternal fire'. I was always aware and somewhat self-conscious of my own physical frailty and fragility that resulted from my near-death experiences with nephritis during the war when I was seven years old and again at 13, and this seems to have urged me also to search for my own purpose or vocation in life.

During a third year in the Sixth form, I took both German and French at Scholarship level. This involved studying vast swathes of literature by Corneille, Racine, Molière, Goethe, Schiller and the German poets of the Romantic Movement. I hid my ignorance fairly well, but never having read any English literature (apart from set books for 'O' level), and not being able to see them in any historical or cross-cultural context, it was pretty clear that I was often way, way out of my depth. In fact, I never read for pleasure, yet surprisingly was regularly called upon to read in public on important occasions and was awarded the Prefects' Reading Prize in my final year (as the best reader from the Bible in Assemblies). I ended up as Deputy-Head Boy and Manager of the School Tuck Shop, selling amongst other things, several hundred warm and sugary jam doughnuts in 15 minutes every breaktime.

At school we received no careers guidance. I do recall one occasion when our Form Master asked us to put up our hands if we were thinking of applying to enter the Civil Service. At the time I didn't know there was any difference between Civil Service and National Service, so I kept quiet. The latter I intended to defer as long as possible. Harry Dawes recommended that I should consider applying for a Choral Scholarship at one of the Oxford Colleges, but I had no idea what that might entail or how to go about it. I did visit Keble College, where I sat an exam for an Exhibition in a room with four sixth formers from Public Schools and I was later interviewed. The one successful candidate I later discovered was, I believe, related to Sir Anthony Eden.

3 SHEFFIELD UNIVERSITY (1954-61)

Had I gained the required two A level passes at Grade B I would have headed for Leeds University, where I had been offered a place; but I just missed out, with a B in German and a C in French. So, at the very last minute, with barely ten days left before the start of the new academic year in 1954, I stood trembling on the doorstep of my fearsome Headmaster's home. In 'Pisser' (Colin) Ewan's study he dictated a letter of application to read for a General Arts degree at Sheffield University. After correcting my spelling of the words 'Yours *truly*' the letter was sealed and posted. A week later I was queuing for interviews with the Staff of various Departments in the main University Hall. I was readily accepted for French and German, but which two other subject Heads would accept me? In the first year one was obliged to study 4 subjects, with a reduction to 3 after one year (provided one was successful in all four at the end of the first year's exams). Failure to pass any one of the 4 at the end of year one meant expulsion. The History Department seemed willing to take me, because I had enjoyed it and gained a very good pass at O level. This had been achieved because of the enthusiasm of the teacher, Mr. Shipley, by learning lists of dates by rote and by the use of mnemonics, all of which ensured factual recall but contributed little to real understanding. But for a fourth subject I crept hesitantly to the Biblical History and Literature Department's desk to be interviewed by Professor F. F. Bruce. Hesitantly, because as an extra subject to fill up my sparse timetable in the Sixth Form I had not only repeated O level Latin (successfully) but also attempted O level Religious Knowledge. With no tuition whatever apart from a weekly five minutes from Bertie Beddis (who popped in to see if I was happily reading Mark's Gospel) and no textbook to work from other than the Bible (AV), I had ended up with the lowest possible Grade of 9 at G.C.E 'O' level. By hiding this information, by stressing that I had been a Sunday School Teacher and was keen and a Confirmed Methodist, remarkably, I was accepted. But only just.

Walking from the Great Hall to the Students' Union I passed the sports noticeboards. I had regularly played hockey on the right wing for the school team, so my attention went straight to the hockey board, where Freshers were invited to add their names if they were interested in joining the University Hockey Club and perhaps having a trial for one of the four University Men's teams. The second column asked for details of Clubs for whom one had previously played, and the third column asked "Position". Having left school in the July of 1954, during the first two weeks of the September I had had a trial and played just one game for Gloucester City 4th XI. Being very competitive and really keen to achieve (trying to make my mark despite my self-conscious frailty), I entered in the second column "Crypt School 1st XI and Gloucester City Hockey Club," and "right or left wing." The next time I looked at the board a few days later, to my utter amazement I found I'd been selected to play on the right wing for the Probables versus the Possibles in a pre-season trial. The game was played on the smoothest pitch I had ever seen, like a bowling green. It was a close-run thing, brought about by ambition, an ambition caused partly, I suspect, by a determination to defy my slender physical frailty and the numerous put-downs I had received because of my weight and thinness over the years. Thus, for four seasons, somewhat to my surprise, but greatly to my pride and enjoyment, I played on the right or left wing, usually for the First XI (gaining University Half Colours), and just occasionally for the Seconds. I toured Holland with the team and also played in the North of England six-a-side knock-out tournament at Bridlington, where we reached the final (which we narrowly lost, but in which I scored a goal whilst being marked by F.H.V.Davis, who had represented England at left-back.).

Academically, the moment of truth came with the end of the first-year exams in 1955. Playing hockey twice a week, sometimes travelling by coach as far afield as Durham and Birmingham, meant that a lot of lectures were missed. Involvement in 'Methsoc' on Wednesdays and Sundays, and attendance every Saturday night at the Union 'Hop' meant that only work that had to be handed in by a certain date was completed. Everything was last minute. For History in particular one needed to do a great deal of reading around the subject. To my recollection I had never read for pleasure. Unsurprisingly the results showed I had passed in everything except History, for which I gained 38%, whereas the pass mark was 40%. Re-sits for those with less than 40% took place every September, a week before the start of the new academic year. Thus, for the entire 1957 Summer holiday I worked in an upstairs room at my sister's home (to be away from distractions and particularly from my father who might have suspected I was being idle), reading, making notes, trying to memorise and understand something of the history of Europe in the 17th and 18th centuries. All this work resulted in a mere 3% improvement in marks gained. It was an extremely close-run thing, but sufficient; I was still at university and no longer had to do History, which was a huge relief.

In year two there arose an opportunity to visit Germany again. The University had an arrangement with the University of Münster in Westphalia for a small number of students studying German on the Honours or Dual Honours courses to spend one Semester there at the expense of the German Government. In my Second Year the number of eligible German Honours students was one short, and so this place was vacant and was made available to anyone interested who happened to be on the General Degree Course. I immediately expressed an interest, ignoring the amount of catching up that would be required in my other two subjects upon my return. I was delighted to be chosen to go. It was a chance to spread my wings and have a good time. Being British made one quite popular in Germany amongst the students, for by 1956 most Germans were fully aware of how misguided and evil their nation had been and how magnanimous and gracious the allied forces had been in victory. Being a non-drinker at that time meant that I didn't join in the crowds of lads who regularly frequented the Pinkus Mueller. I shared a hostel room with Hans Bloth, a disillusioned member of one of the various student Verbindungen. However, I soon learnt that not everyone could be trusted, how inadvisable it was to hitch-hike on one's own, and how useful it was to have a link with BAOR

Münster (where I went to play tennis at weekends with the Army Chaplain, Rev Christian and to exchange Deutschmarks for NAAFI baffs, to buy British comfort food). I also learnt how strong my attachment to the Christian Church was. I worshipped in Münster in the Lutheran Church and listened to preachers such as the renowned Pastor Martin Niemoeller, who had spent years in Dachau Concentration Camp for preaching against Nazism. On my return to Sheffield six months later I soon learned also how much work I had missed in French and in 'Bibs' (Biblical History and Literature) whilst I'd been away and had to rely heavily on copying other people's notes, which inevitably meant less to me than it did to them.

Despite this, straight after I returned, I was pleased to be nominated and elected as President of the very flourishing University Methodist Society. It was a very close-run election, but once in office I soon discovered that the work involved was very time-consuming. Regular Wednesday evening meetings were planned and held at Sheffield Victoria Hall in term-time, with some very distinguished speakers, whom at weekly meetings I was to introduce as President. Among the speakers were national figures including George Thomas, later to become Lord Tonypandy and Speaker of the House of Commons, and famous Hyde Park soap-box speaker Rev. Dr. Donald Soper, who also became a Lord. The world-renowned former internee of Dachau, Pastor Martin Niemöller also came to speak, whom I had earlier heard preach in Münster. Following the Sunday evening services at the Victoria Hall students were always invited to the Chaplain's home, where Rev Brian's O'Gorman's wife's hospitality gained the Society the reputation of being a kind of marriage bureau, for so many love affairs sprang from it. There we chatted, consumed a lot of biscuits and tea, and sang a lot of hymns in four-part harmony, which I occasionally accompanied on the piano.

Being a last-minute swatter, when the final exams came, I spent nine hours every day for six weeks in the Sheffield City library reading, summarizing and learning my notes from the previous two years. I allowed myself two weeks of revision for each of my three subjects. To my surprise it paid off better than I had expected, with a General Arts Degree, First Division Pass. Not ever having received any careers guidance, and not knowing about any other occupation, I drifted onto the Education Course, completed successful teaching practice placements at High Stores Grammar and Wath-on-Dearn Grammar Schools and gained my Diploma in Education. I travelled to these far-flung schools each day and in all weathers on a little old Corgi motor bike that my Gloucester girlfriend's lodger had given me, having herself found it very unsuitable.

Apart from my first month in Sheffield and the Semester spent in Germany in Münster I lived in digs at the home of Miss Ethel Bromley in Earl Marshal Road, Firvale. She charged £2-17-6d for half board on five days of the week and full board at weekends. This was reduced to £2-10shillings when I had to share a bedroom with my Geordie dig-mate Frank Wilkinson. For this sum we received not only the half board for five days and full board at weekends, but 'Brom' also did all our washing and ironing and let us use her telephone free of charge.

Prior to my final teaching practice at the beginning of March 1958 I plucked up the courage to approach the most beautiful girl in Methsoc. and asked her if she would come out with me on a date. I had been cheekily rude to this

Wendy Pepperell several months earlier at the Freshers' Bazaar when I first set eyes on her. I was manning the Methodist Society's stall with others when she approached. I recall asking her name and where she came from. On learning that she was Wendy from Cardiff, I replied "Oh, my father's got a cow called Wendy!" With such a potentially offensive chat-up line, it is not surprising that I was cautious. My invitation to her to join me for a last celebration of freedom prior to my final teaching practice was, to my great delight, met with some interest. However, the date I suggested, March 1st, turned out to be her 19th birthday, and she had already bought tickets to take a friend called Mary Friend to the Sheffield City Hall to hear the Halle Orchestra, where Grieg's Piano Concerto was being performed. A few days later Wendy told me that Mary had offered to let me go in her place. Thus, our first date involved me being taken out to the second classical music concert of my life, on Wendy's birthday, and at her expense. (The first had been in Germany when my hosts in Düsseldorf had taken me to a performance of the Messiah, sung in German).

I immediately let my secret Gloucester girlfriend of the previous five or six years know that I had fallen in love with Wendy, and this brought a swift end to that relationship. It had needed to be kept secret, as my father would have been strongly disapproving and very suspicious of what we might be getting up to. He would certainly have threatened to stop supporting me financially at university, as he had on one previous occasion. His disapproval taught me the art and skills needed for clever deception, which I had had to cultivate and practice on a regular basis when at home.

From March 1st to June in 1958 was the time of rapturously falling in love. The thought of knowing that they would be committing themselves to a lifetime's role as a Minister's wife would inevitably have put many girls off. Yet Wendy seemed even to be enthused at the idea. My father had always stressed the importance of not getting in any position of falling in love on the grounds that it would promote what he called 'affection', a term which sounded as if it had a sinful connotation. He probably meant 'lust'. Discovering for myself at last what affection really meant was a time of sheer ecstasy and euphoria; so much so, that within six weeks I 'popped the question' in Concord Park, Sheffield, and to my great delight her immediate response was in the affirmative. In fact, so euphoric was I that, on getting engaged, I completely lost my appetite and was off all food for about four days, living on pure adrenaline or something.

Like several other members of 'Methsoc' at Sheffield, inspired by the ministry of Rev. Brian O'Gorman at Sheffield Central Hall, I had begun to feel called strongly to the Ministry of the Methodist Church for several years. To my delight Wendy was not put off by it. In fact, she was greatly supportive and very encouraging. At very short notice I applied first to become a Local (Lay) Preacher and secondly to candidate for the Methodist Ministry. In view of my Biblical Studies at Sheffield I was exempted from Local Preachers' exams and from some Ministerial Candidates' papers on Old and New Testament, which is just as well. I only had to be examined on Christian Doctrine. With no time at all to study the prescribed texts properly, it is something of a miracle that I managed narrowly to scrape through.

The interviews for the Ministry always took place at the Methodist 'July Committee'. In 1954 they were held, conveniently, in the John Wesley's 'New Room' in Bristol. My interview was also a close-run thing, for it was clear that I was regarded as a graduate candidate from a somewhat protected background; "Mr Lane, can you describe for us the meaning of 'grace'", asked one. Silence. I hadn't really studied the main textbook on Christian doctrine. (Reading never was my strong point.) "Mr. Lane, have you ever met a thug?" asked another elderly churchman in gaiters. It was certainly touch and go. Years later, if I had met the panel again, I would certainly have been able to assure them that I had certainly met more thugs than they had.

ONLY JUST

4 DIDSBURY METHODIST THEOLOGICAL COLLEGE, BRISTOL (1958-61)

The College was an all-male community of about fifty or sixty students. Women had not yet been admitted to the Ministry of the Church.

It was usual for Ministerial candidates who already had University degrees to be designated to do their training at Wesley House in Cambridge. In 1958 however there were so many such candidates that a number of us were sent to study for 3 years at Didsbury Methodist Theological College in Bristol, which was affiliated to Bristol University. By August Wendy and I had got engaged and had been going out together for almost 6 months. We wanted to be together, and so she applied successfully to do teacher training in Bristol at Redland Training College. At Didsbury, in addition to lectures in Church History and Pastoralia we were expected to take a BA Honours Course in Theology at Bristol University. This involved learning Greek and Hebrew, which I confess I found difficult and regarded as rather pointless. I would have preferred to do a thesis, do something practical in the wider community or produce a German Grammar for theological students, but that was not an option. Hockey occasionally for Bristol University and Football for the College also featured prominently in my weekly routine and got me out of College more frequently than was the case for most theological students.

The freedom I had enjoyed at University in Sheffield was not available at Didbury, where rather strict rules were imposed on all students. Everyone was expected to attend prayers before breakfast and each evening. Students were only allowed out of College on a maximum of five evenings per term, and that was on the expectation that they would return before 10 p.m. Lectures were on five mornings each week from 9 a.m. until lunch at 1 o'clock. Those of us who were studying on the University theological degree course spent most of each morning at lectures in the University. At Didbury however we could entertain visitors in our rooms, but only on Saturday afternoons until tea-time at 5 o'clock. On Sundays we were usually sent off to take Church services far and wide around Bristol, into Somerset and parts of South Wales. I often travelled to these appointments on my old Ambassador 197 motorbike, which was not well maintained; the headlights were very poor, and finding remote country Chapels was often a nightmare. Sometimes Wendy accompanied me on the pillion seat (with no crash helmet). Students would often return late in the evening and found little, or no food left out for us, but it was not unknown for students to raid Matron's supplies set aside for the Staff.

On the positive side however, the quality of the lectures we received in Didbury was very good and enlightening, delivered by four outstanding men, Rev's Fred Greeves (theology and pastoralia), Rupert Davies (Church history), Kenneth Grayston (Greek and New Testament) and Dai Isthwyn Blythin (Hebrew and Old Testament). What I subsequently found was lacking was any work experience and any broadening of experience to encounter worship and leadership from within other Christian denominations; for example, on moving as a Probationary Minister to my first Churches I was at the great disadvantage of having never in my life attended a funeral, a situation that I swiftly had to remedy. Training in conducting business meetings was provided in the fact that twice each week after lunch a Student Business Meeting was held, which all students had to attend, and each student had to take the Chair in turns and ensure that true business procedures were followed in the correct constitutional manner, following the guidelines printed in the thick "Constitutional Practice and Discipline of the Methodist Church". This twice-weekly meeting was called "Seats", and the general aim of all in attendance was to cause problems for whoever was chairing the meeting. These gatherings were extremely enjoyable and quite hilarious for everyone apart from whoever was Chairman on that occasion; but it was excellent training for later life and work.

Another worthwhile institution was the system of daily tea clubs held after lunch, into which we were placed and in which we remained for three years. This meant no student was left out of a friendly social group and ensured we gained wonderful colleagues and friends for life to whom we could and did often turn for guidance, reassurance or simply friendship.

In my third year, by a narrow margin, I was elected as College Student Chairman. Again, it was a close-run thing; but my fellow students must have believed in my ability to control their business meetings and represent them reasonably well. Being College Chairman involved representing the College on many and various important occasions (including speaking at Clubland in London on the same stage as the actor Richard Attenborough, and preaching at Kingswood School), chairing major Student Community gatherings, leading the College Student Committee and sitting next to the Principal, Rev. Dr Fred Greeves on top table every day at dinner throughout my final year. The end result was that I only just managed, by the skin of my teeth, to scrape through my theology finals in 1961 with an Honours degree. It was, I'm afraid, another case of 'only just'. I managed the Hebrew paper by learning off by heart large swathes of the Second Book of Kings in English, and the Greek by similarly learning many chapters of the set Epistle.

Another close-run thing was the fact that until 1961, unless one was in full time education, all young men under the age of 26 were conscripted for National Service. My 26th birthday was in the month I left Didsbury College and moved to my first appointment as a Probationary Methodist Minister. I thus 'only just' avoided conscription into the armed forces, a fact of which Wendy has occasionally reminded me has been somewhat to my disadvantage and detriment, particularly when I have been slow to assist with housework or proved to be untidy, disorganized, undomesticated or impractical.

5 METHODIST CIRCUIT MINISTER

The moment when any year group of Methodist Theological Students left College was felt to be the appropriate time for them to get married. By 1958 married students had only recently been admitted to the College for the first time. Those not yet married were expected to wait until they had completed their courses. By marrying on leaving College, Ministers would head for their first 'station' with their recently acquired wife. During the final year at College one had to opt to serve at home or overseas, or to leave the decision to the Church. At first, after talking with Wendy, I hinted at the latter, whereupon I was asked if the Luknow and Banares District of North India might be a place where Wendy and I might feel called to serve. Years later, when in our sixties, we eventually visited Banares, now called Varanasi, on the Ganges, and we concluded that we would certainly not have been well suited in that particular environment if we had agreed to be sent there. We would not have lasted long.

Within a few weeks of our first date on March 1st, 1958, Wendy and I had got engaged. I had proposed in the appropriately named "Concord Park", Sheffield (on the pitch-and-putt golf course) whilst it was getting dark. Thus, began not only my appreciation of classical music that she introduced me to, but also an engagement that seemed an eternity. Although baptized in the Anglican Church, Wendy grew up attending Roath Park Methodist Church in Cardiff, which was situated just at the end of the road where she lived. It was a Wesleyan Methodist Church until Methodist Union in 1932 but it kept the Wesleyan tradition of regular Morning Prayer (like many an Anglican Church). It was wonderful to have found someone with such a delightful, pleasing disposition. We shared the same faith, we were deeply in love, and it was clear from her gregarious, smiling nature that she would prove to be a joy to live with and a great blessing to the congregations to whom I would be sent to minister.

On asking her father if I could marry his beautiful 19 year-old younger daughter, his reaction was, "You poor devil"; whereas, to start with, my father's response, as we met him at the Lonsdale Road Methodist Garden Party, was "On condition that…. ." Then he withdrew any condition. I was 23 by that time and we couldn't marry for a further 3 years in any case because of Church regulations. Dad had always been keen to ensure that I didn't follow my brother's example. Sebert had got married at the age of about 19 or 20 whilst doing his National Service. Our parents had been in my opinion, understandably but unreasonably distressed at this, so Rev Gordon Scott who was officiating at the service in Enfield had driven three of us in father's car with our mother weeping next to me on the back seat, assuming the marriage would be a disaster. Seventy-three years later she would be surprised and relieved to know that it is still going strong. It was this same Minister whom I, at the age of 16, had consulted because of my constant need to deceive my parents, which, looking back, must have worried me greatly (because of the fear of being caught and what might follow), who had told me straight: "Your father has a warped mind." Sadly, I had to agree with him; and our mother was never able to express an opinion and always had to be submissive to him and his views.

At the same time as I had moved to Didsbury College in Bristol, we had managed to arrange things in 1958 so that Wendy also moved from Sheffield to Bristol where she began a two-year teacher training course at Redland College, Bristol, followed by a year teaching at a very rough Secondary School on the Southmead Estate. This was very convenient, although the Didsbury College rules stipulated that a student was only allowed out of College for a maximum of five evenings per term, and even then we had to be back in College by 10 o'clock! Furthermore, we were not expected to get married until after having completed the three- or four-year theological course.

Our wedding took place at Roath Park Methodist Church, Cardiff, on 29th July 1961 and was led by Rev. Dr. Ron Ashman and the Didsbury College New Testament Lecturer and Vice-Principal Rev. Kenneth Grayston. Wendy entered the Church to the singing of "Christ is made the sure foundation" to the tune Westminster Abbey. "Love diving, all loves excelling" and "Captain of Israel's host" were the other hymns chosen. On the strict expectation of my parents the reception was a non-alcoholic event. It was held in the Church Hall and consisted mainly of a salad. My father was inclined towards fits of impetuous generosity. Thus, having in mind the future needs of our Ministerial work for the Church, my parents generously gave us a brand-new Morris

1000 as a wedding present. So off we drove on honeymoon, (emptying the car of confetti on Brecon Beacons), first to Builth Wells, then Llandrindod Wells and on to Harlech, where we got badly sun-burnt and were the only non-golfers staying in the golfing hotel. A second, more convivial wedding reception apparently took place at 45 Bangor Street soon after we and the 'total abstainers' had all left the wedding. This swift departure also accorded with the suggestion of our Principal, Rev. Dr. Fred Greeves, in one of his Pastoralia lectures, that the length of time that we ought to suggest to young couples that should elapse between the start of the Church service and a couple's departure from the reception for their honeymoon should be no more than three hours. "Any longer, and the guests might become restless," he had said. How things have changed!

Stonehouse

The Methodist Conference 'stationed 'me as a Probationer Minister, with a dispensation to administer the Sacraments, in the Dursley & Stonehouse Circuit in Gloucestershire. Two years in Stonehouse, looking after five Methodist village Churches (Stonehouse, Eastington, Leonard Stanley, Halmore and Whitminster) and their congregations were demanding for both of us. Ministers had no allocated weekly 'day off', Sabbaticals had not yet been invented, and we were allowed three Sundays off per year. The car was invaluable, as the Churches were widely scattered across the Severn Plain.

One quite primitive hamlet community 15 miles away lived in a time warp at Halmore. Slimbridge was probably the nearest village to Halmore. Most of the members of the elderly community had no means of transport of their own; and there was no public transport apart from a barge on the

Gloucester to Sharpness Canal about two miles' walk away. I tried regularly to visit the village every Thursday afternoon, but when I did, it was rather essential to call on every Church member to prevent any accusation of favouritism. Next door to the Chapel lived old Mr and Mrs Mears who served as Caretakers and Church Treasurers. They kept the Church collections in a metal box up their chimney, which they expected me to check once a quarter. With the old range keeping the cottage warm, they both suffered from chilblains in the winter. Mr Mears was convinced that the best remedy was, unlike bathing the feet in water and permanganate of potash, as I had done as a child, but to walk through the village, break a sprig from a holly tree and, on returning home, to beat his bare feet with it until they bled. He also believed that the best way to treat his bad back was by drinking a drop of Sloanes' Liniment, because he felt it better to push the pain (and the chilblains) out from within, rather than by following the instructions and thus rubbing the pain in by massage. I as Minister was also expected to act as auctioneer after their mid-week Harvest Service, and woe betide me if I ever allowed an item to be sold for less than someone had paid for it or for less than it was worth. I once returned five minutes after leaving and walked into a very heated row.

Ministerial stipends are paid only four times per year. My first quarter's pay cheque was £96 which had to last 13 weeks. This income was supplemented in a very small way by the fact that I was also Assistant Chaplain at Wycliffe College, which involved preparing boys at the Wycliffe Prep School for their Common Entrance Exam in Religious Knowledge and conducting occasional Communion Services for boys from Methodist families. Wendy had been advised at an evening for fiancées at College that, to survive on such a meagre stipend, Ministers' wives might have to learn to cut their husbands' hair and make a breast of lamb last a whole family for two days. The winter of 1963 was the coldest for decades. With cautious thrift and meticulous housekeeping, we somehow survived, thanks to Wendy managing the house and obtaining several brief supply teaching jobs. The first funeral I had to conduct was of a young lad in Eastington who, believing that the police were after him, took his own life by putting his head in the gas oven at home. Prior to leaving College I had never attended a funeral in my life, so a few weeks earlier I had decided to attend the funeral of a complete stranger at a Church in Cardiff and had taken notes. Apart from lectures on Pastoral matters and regular preaching engagements in far-flung places there had been no work experience placements for those of us who had been on the degree course.

The 'Eastington and Leonard Stanley Youth Project', prepared by my predecessors Tom Nicholas and Irvine Vincent, came to fruition soon after our arrival in the Circuit, with 'Open' Youth Clubs being established in the Methodist Church 'schoolrooms' in both villages. The Churches provided the premises, the Local Education Authority paid for the full-time leader, and I chaired the Management Committee. The best candidate, Bert Jones (from Frodsham NCH Home), was appointed as Youth Leader. He had a wife, three very young daughters, no money and nowhere to live. As a temporary measure my father generously lent them a 22 ft. Berkeley caravan which he parked alongside the Eastington Chapel. It was not insured. Whilst the family was out one day, the clothing in an airing cupboard caught fire. The caravan went up in flames and everything was lost. My parents bore the financial loss of the caravan. That was another close shave. Countless generous Church members across the Circuit came to the rescue in many ways and the Project survived, with the County Council eventually providing the family with a house to rent.

During those two years of our first appointment, every Sunday evening our lounge was filled with young people, where we held a lively Youth Fellowship. We borrowed a film projector and often showed films, leading to discussion. We led a large party of the Youth Fellowship members together with the young people from those two village youth clubs of Eastington and Leonard Stanley to St. Ives for a week's holiday in the Summer of 1962. It was particularly memorable on three counts; firstly, Wendy was pregnant, secondly the huge quantity of beef that Wendy had ordered on our very limited budget for the Sunday meal was found to have gone rancid by the Sunday because we had no fridge and it was hot weather; thirdly, I had to send one lad home alone on the train for getting himself very drunk.

We were also invited by the Stroud/Duderstadt Twinning Committee in 1963 to lead a large party of students and police cadets from Stroud to Duderstadt, a town in the German Harz mountains right on the border of what at that time was 'East Germany'. This trip was also long remembered because of the explosions we heard every night, caused by animals setting off mines in the no-man's-land between East and West, and the fact that the entire party was taken violently ill following a meal in a Youth Hostel. That night, in the Youth Hostel we were all locked in for the night in our dormitories with very little light and were not allowed to depart next morning until, with mops and cold water, we had cleaned the place up. Wendy and I paid a most interesting visit to the home of the Lutheran Pastor, who surprised us by explaining the classes he ran for

Confirmands. He required them each to learn by heart 50 passages of Scripture and 50 hymns. He explained that they lived in an area of very great tension, just less than 200 metres from the double fence which constituted the Iron Curtain, and he could well recall their need for Church supplies when, under Nazi rule, all their Church books had been destroyed.

Whilst in this our first appointment Julian was born during the extremely cold March of 1963 in the Stroud Maternity Hospital. Husbands were not allowed to be present at the birth in those days, so I had to leave Wendy on a bed in the Hospital corridor, where she remained all day. After a safe delivery she was expected to remain in hospital for a very tedious 10 days. That was normal. I never drove more slowly and with greater care in my life than on the drive home from the hospital. It was in Stonehouse that Wendy learnt to drive and passed her driving test. We survived the long freezing Winter of 1963.

Our two memorable years in the Dursley and Stonehouse Circuit were soon up. We had been introduced to a life of genteel poverty, in which there was no allowance for a weekly day off; Sabbaticals for Methodist Ministers did not yet exist, and we were permitted three Sundays off each year for possible holidays. In those days Manses were furnished mainly with 'throw-outs' from Church members' homes, so on the day before departure, never having yet heard of the phrases 'global warming' or 'air pollution' we lit an enormous bonfire in the small back garden of St Cyril's Lodge to burn a very shabby sofa that had been donated by a very well-meaning elderly Church member.

ONLY JUST

Stafford

Ordination in 1963 at the (perhaps appropriately named) Raikes Parade Methodist Church in Blackpool was followed by our next appointment, which was in Stafford, where we lived for six very eventful years. There Clare and Carys were born, both of them being home births, for they were widely encouraged at that time. It was claimed to be more natural. In fact, it was almost certainly to save the NHS money. Clare's delivery was very swift indeed and straightforward, whereas Carys's was quite the opposite, with the witch-like midwife shouting "get me a b----- doctor". There was no response from the Doctor's home telephone, so I raced out in search and found his wife working in their garden; but in vain, for I was told he was tending patients in the prison and was incommunicado. (Mobile phones did not exist.) Mercifully, on my return to the Manse, Carys was soon safely delivered. The doctor arrived three hours after the birth, smiling that things had apparently "gone smoothly."

The Church at Rising Brook was modern and on a sound financial footing, having been one of the first in the country to introduce Planned Giving under the charismatic leadership of Rev Jack Puntis. His successor only lasted two years and, whilst he married a local girl from Weston-upon-Trent, did not really suit what was required. It was also an outward-looking Church with strong, young, male leadership and with a progressive ethos. 'Service to the surrounding community' was its watchword, and that community, much of it from Birmingham 'overspill', consisted of a large Council Estate and another estate owned by the English Electric Company. Rather than spending money on an organ, the Church preferred to use a grand piano and spend its income on service to the community locally, as well as on worthy causes abroad. Wendy and I established an open Toddlers Club for 25 children, which ran on five mornings each week and had a volunteer staff of five, led by Wendy herself. From this there grew a very lively and thriving Young Wives Group. The Sunday School also grew in size, as also did the Youth Club and Sunday night Youth Fellowship in the Manse. My other charges included the Methodist Churches at Acton Gate, Hixon and Weston-upon-Trent. Soon I was appointed District Youth Secretary for the Wolverhampton and Shewsbury District, a position in addition to running the four Churches, which involved a lot of travelling, for the District stretched as far west as Aberystwyth.

As District Youth Secretary I was appointed as a Representative to attend the first Official Consultation between the Methodist Church of Great Britain and the Roman Catholic Church, held at Westminster Cathedral. Cardinal Heenan memorably opened the conference with the assurance that Catholics and Methodists had one particular common characteristic, namely a deep personal love of our Lord Jesus Christ. As a young child I had once dared to ask my father if it was better to be a Catholic than nothing at all, and he admitted that he didn't know and suggested I ask the Minister. I don't remember if I did; but my admiration for many aspects the Catholic Church was changed at Westminster that day, and in later years resulted in interesting exchanges with several Catholic Priests in St Malo.

I was also at that time appointed as Chaplain to Rev Brian O'Gorman during his tenure as President of the U.K. Methodist Conference. When he went on his official visit to attend the Annual Conference in Belfast of the Irish Methodist Church, I accompanied him and was called upon to address a vast rally of young Methodists. It was right at the start of the 'Troubles'.

It was whilst attending a Meeting in Wolverhampton of the District Youth Committee in the lounge at the home of the Chairman, Rev Brian O'Gorman that something very strange occurred. I was present as the Committee's Secretary. Another meeting was taking place in Brian's dining room, and I spotted someone walking up the path to join those in the dining room whom I suddenly thought I recognized. I found it impossible to concentrate on the business we were discussing, because all the time I was trying to recall precisely what had happened to this man. Where had I seen him before? Then it dawned on me. He had once, perhaps twice, attended Meth Soc in Sheffield. "But isn't he the one", I puzzled, "who strangely disappeared, presumed drowned at sea?" Hadn't his clothes been found on a beach somewhere? I had read it in a national newspaper or heard it on the radio. I began to think I could recall his name. At that moment I was the only person in the world who realized he was probably still alive. Surely not! After the meeting I told Brian why I had not participated in the meeting in any way and suggested he find his old Visitors Book from his Sheffield days. There was the name! Brian had heard of the tragic disappearance of the man to whom I referred, but said that the person in the next room had a different name. "Well, he must have changed his identity, because I've always been good at recognizing faces", I replied, and Brian believed me. I left it in his hands. He phoned the police, and the next day we heard that he had been arrested. He had deserted his wife and three children, and his mother had died believing him to be dead. His father was still alive, - a Supernumerary Methodist Minister.

It was during our time in Stafford that I was chosen to

represent young Methodist Ministers at a week-long conference in the German Democratic Republic (East Germany) at a town close to the Polish border called Storkow. It was held in German and was attended by Protestant Ministers from many countries. Instead of arriving at Check Point Charlie in Berlin I flew via Amsterdam to the East German Schonfeld Airport, where I was not expected, so I was kept in what looked like a cattle pen for several hours and was searched. The border police took from me my Bible and my copy of the Sunday Times. The former was eventually returned to me. Eventually I was met and driven off but had to report regularly to the Police in Storkow.

Financially life at home continued to be extremely difficult in the Manse. The coke boiler and the car became increasingly more expensive to run. To make ends meet we took in a lodger for a while. As soon as Carys was born, we became for a while eligible for Supplementary Benefit from the State. To help out I took up a part-time teaching post at Stafford Girls' High School (German and Sixth form R.E. discussions) and also did occasional supply work at the King Edward VI Boys' Grammar School, teaching what was then known as Religious Knowledge. Increasingly I felt drawn as much in the direction of Education as I did towards serving the Church. Child-centred 'Experiential' learning was in vogue at the time, and the subject once called Religious Knowledge (i.e. Scripture Knowledge) was becoming Religious Education introducing awareness of other world religions. I applied for posts in Teacher Training Colleges and for Chaplaincies at Methodist Public Schools. At one of the former I was offered a job on condition that I would still take up the position even if the Church said that as an ordained Minister I could not do so. This offer I declined. At Shebbear Methodist Public School I was offered the

Chaplaincy, but fortunately was persuaded by the Rising Brook Church Leaders not to leave them at such short notice. This proved to be a merciful escape, for a good friend from Didsbury College days, Rev Graham Haslam, who later took up the position at Shebbear, found it to be a huge disappointment, for apparently the Chaplain's roll was held in low esteem and was treated as cheap labour (teaching full time yet being paid on a Minister's stipend). An invitation also came from the Methodist Missionary Society for me to consider accepting the role of Headmaster at the French speaking Nouveau College Bird in Port au Prince, Haiti. With a young family, after we had watched the film based on Grahame Green's book 'The Comedians', accompanied by a Haitian nurse called Pennycook (who verified the horrors depicted in the film), we concluded that such a relocation, with three young children, during the rule of President Papa Doc would be extremely undesirable and unwise. Three or four years later in Guernsey I came to know the widow and taught the son of a Methodist Minister who, about to take his family back with him to Haiti, had tragically taken his own life. Nonetheless, I still hoped I would succeed in finding a position in which I could combine a penchant for Education with my commitment to the Church. With nothing materializing, our six years of intensive and fulfilling work in Stafford came to an end.

Abingdon

An invitation came to become Minister at Trinity Church in Abingdon in 1969, where I was also to become Officiating Chaplain at RAF Abingdon. The Church was a combined Methodist/United Reformed Church, with two Ministers working in partnership. My U.R.C. colleague was the young and very gifted Rev. Dr. Colin Thompson. He had obtained a doctorate for his thesis in Spanish on 'The theology of St John of the Cross', which he had submitted with success both to the Spanish and to the Theology Departments at Oxford. Again, income from student lodgers helped to pay our bills, but the major change came when Wendy retrained in Oxford to teach Primary Age children and then taking up a post at St. Edmunds R.C. School. To make this possible, whilst Julian and Clare now both went to Carswell School, Carys attended two different playschools, one quite genteel gathering in St Michael's Church Hall and the other an RAF Playgroup which she remembers as being 'rather rough'. To the apparent disappointment of the congregation, our stay in Abingdon lasted only 2 years.

The change from a church with a clear vision of planned giving and service to the community, located on two estates, where we had been involved with many dozens of young families, to a church in more leafy suburbia, came as quite a surprise.

One lifelong joy sprang from our first week, when we received a very simple act of kindness. Abingdon's Churches in 1969 were ecumenically minded. Twenty yards from Trinity was St Michael's High Anglican Church, one of whose members, Glenys Enticott left us a note offering to babysit. When Wendy called to thank her, to their surprise, they found they had been at school together in Cardiff. Glenys and John (Abingdon's Christian Aid Rep) had three children of similar ages to ours. As lifelong friends we have spent countless holidays together in Guernsey, Eastbourne, Anglesey, Brittany, Crete, Skiathos and cruised the Yangtse and the Dnieper.

6 THE MOVE TO EDUCATION

By regularly taking School Assemblies in Abingdon schools, I soon spotted in one of their Staff Rooms an advertisement in the Times Educational Supplement for the Post of Anglican Chaplain of Elizabeth College and Priest-in-Charge of the Church of St. James the Less in Guernsey. Undeterred I sent off a letter of application.

It happened to be at the time in 1970 when a scheme (familiarly known as the 'Conversations') had been drawn up whereby the Church of England and the Methodist Church might become re-united after 200 years of separation. Many people including me expected the scheme to be accepted both by the Anglican General Synod and by the Methodist Conference. Amongst these, fortunately, was the Principal of Elizabeth College, Mr. J. K. Day (affectionately known as Jake). He was a keen ecumenist and a staunch supporter of what was known as the 'Conversations'. He held Methodism in very high regard and was conscious of the fact that many of his students came from strong Methodist backgrounds. He interviewed us over a meal in an Abingdon restaurant by the Thames and at the end of the meal said that he would like to appoint me, subject to the various Church authorities agreeing to it. The Bishop of Winchester let him know that he thought it would be an appropriate ecumenical appointment, and Rev. Rupert Davies (my Church History Tutor at Didsbury College, wartime Chaplain of Kingswood School and President of the Methodist Conference that year) supported it wholeheartedly.

Whilst negotiations went on, Jake held the fort for a year, with help from local clergy. My predecessor at Elizabeth College, Rev. Alan Charters, had already moved back to the U.K. in July 1970 and became Headmaster at the Kings School in Gloucester. However, it soon became clear that major hazards stood in the way of my taking up the appointment in Guernsey. One of these was the opposition of certain local Anglican clergy to the idea of a Methodist Minister as Chaplain of a College that had a Church of England foundation. (Queen Elizabeth the First had founded it in 1563 to provide French-speaking Priests for the Church of England for the territories she ruled in the north of France). A few priests already held a certain antagonism towards the College by virtue of the fact that some Parish Churches had occasionally lost their best young choristers together with their families when their sons had joined the College. The excellent Choir at St. James, under Eric Waddams, was regarded as having "stolen" them. St James the Less also had debts resulting from the war-time Nazi Occupation and the use of the Church for Lutheran Services by the German Occupying Forces, during which time the building had been poorly maintained. The house that normally went with the job needed to be sold if the Church were to remain open, in order to pay for repairs. Time slipped by. The Principal himself took the Boarders' Sunday Services and some of the Divinity lessons (with the help of one or two local clergy) for a year. He again approached me on 26th January 1971 firmly offering me the position, despite the fact that it would be unlikely that a house could be offered to us. I accepted his offer, and we shook hands, he having obtained the agreement of the College Visitor (the Bishop of Winchester) and I having got the President of the Conference (one of my former College lecturers, Rev. Rupert Davies) to intercede with the Bishop on my behalf. I gave in my notice to the Church in Abingdon and the Church took action to find a successor. However, unexpectedly, Mr. Day surprised us by arriving again on the doorstep of our Abingdon Manse on March 1st, 1971. It happened to be Wendy's 32nd birthday. He explained that he unfortunately had to ask me to withdraw my acceptance of the position because of "complications". He had clearly been put under enormous pressure by Guernsey's Dean, who admitted that he had been put "in an impossible position by the local clergy." "St James the Less is to be closed", he said.

I explained to Mr. Day that I had already resigned my position in Abingdon and that the process of finding my successor was well underway. I fetched him a pen and a sheet of writing paper and asked him to put in writing what he had previously offered me in January. This he very kindly did, much to my great relief. It was another very close-run thing, another 'only just' experience. Two weeks later I received a letter from the Dean of Guernsey, The Very Rev. Fred Cogman, dated 12th March 1971, confirming my appointment.

I had already been elected by the District Synod as a representative of the Oxford and Leicester District to the Methodist Conference in Birmingham in July of that year (1971) when, full of optimism, the Conference gave the required two thirds majority in favour of accepting the "Conversations" (which would have resulted in the re-uniting of the Methodist Church and the Church of England), only for the Conference, minutes later, to be utterly stunned and dismayed on learning of the voting at the General Synod of the Church of England. Whilst the Bishops and the Laity by a large majority had accepted the Report and Proposals contained in the "Conversations", the Clergy, by an unlikely alliance between Anglo-Catholics and Evangelicals, failed by the narrowest of margins to give the necessary two thirds majority in favour of the scheme. (Evangelicals had said that in the proposed Service of Reconciliation it should not be necessary to have any laying on of hands by Bishops on Methodist Ministers' heads. Anglo-Catholics on the other hand had insisted that such laying of hands on Methodist Ministers by Bishops was not only essential, but must indeed be regarded as a re-ordination). In a sense therefore, I was to become something of an anomaly in my position as a Methodist Chaplain of an Anglican Direct Grant Public School for the next nine years.

Subsequent letters informed me that the Church of St James the Less would shortly close and the Vicarage would be sold. A further letter arrived nonetheless from the Bishop, written on August 2nd, 1971 welcoming us to the Island and outlining how the appointment might work out.

The Methodist Conference of 1971 granted me permission to take up the post as a 'Sector Minister' serving this 'outside organisation'; yet it seemed strange that although other Ministers arrived to serve the Methodist Church in September of that year I was not included in their service of welcome. It was as if the Methodist Church in Guernsey did not regard my serving as Chaplain of a School with an

Anglican foundation (and teaching full time there) as being a legitimate form of Christian outreach into the community. Nonetheless I immediately started conducting Church Services (between 20 and 30 each year) in the two Methodist Circuits that existed at that time and continued to do so for the next fifty years.

With no accommodation available, it was thanks to a gift from my parents that we were able to put a deposit down on a house in Bailiff's Cross Road. We changed its name from 'Bardon Lea' to 'Maison des Ruettes.' The purchase price was £6,850, and I took up the appointment as Chaplain on September 1st on an annual salary scale of £1,210 to £1,950 per annum, plus £222 as Head of the Divinity Department. This was almost double what my stipend as a Methodist Circuit Minister had been. Masters' sons were admitted to the College free of charge, so Julian started immediately at Elizabeth College Lower School (Beechwood). Wendy took up a temporary post at St. Andrews Primary School, taking Clare and the unregistered four-year-old Carys with her, by kind permission of the Headmaster, Bob Gill. Carys was not put on the roll until old enough. Very soon Wendy moved to Vauvert Infant School where she later became Deputy-Head.

Chaplaincy at the College could no longer be centred around any Church building, and Morning Assemblies had to be held in Spurgeon Chapel or in the College Hall. I led these four mornings each week; on the fifth morning I took Assembly at Elizabeth College Lower School (Beechwood). My position kept me extremely busy seven days a week during term time. There was also Saturday morning school with afternoon sport. Sunday mornings were taken up with either Holy Communion or 'House Prayers' for the Boarders (a 40-minute service in the College Hall) or by accompanying them to St. Stephen's Church for Holy Communion. This was often followed by my going on to conduct a Methodist service in one of the Churches in the two Circuits (English and 'French') on the Island. If I had no further such commitment, the new College Principal, Richard Wheadon, expected me to take coffee with him for at least an hour each week as he unburdened himself of his week's trials and tribulations in strictest confidence.

Elizabeth College (founded 1563)

Elizabeth College had a Lower School (affectionately called 'Beechwood') and Upper School (11-18) three form entry of 90 boys each year at the age of 11. Annually, 26 of these were scholars from the States Primary Schools, having opted for the College and been successful in the 11+ exam. The rest were fee-payers. The Boarding House accommodated around 40 boys, mostly from overseas, plus a few being sons of busy Island hoteliers. Up to the age of sixteen the teaching class sizes were regularly 30.

At the start, as Head of Department I taught all the Divinity throughout the Upper School (apart from a small portion of the Sixth Form 'A' level work involving Church History which I was able to delegate to a local Methodist Minister, Rev Colin Hough). All boys began the O level "Life and Teaching of Jesus Christ" course in the third year (later known as Year 9) and sat the G.C.E. 'O' level exam at the end of the fourth year (year 10). I had already acquired various skills at teaching this particular course whilst at Stafford Girls High School, so I soon found the success rate at the College to be very high. I had broken St Mark's Gospel and the passages from St Matthew into about 20 themes, which the students found helpful. However, once successful, all boys began studying AS level Religious Studies in their fifth year (year 11). It soon became obvious to me that the prescribed subject matter (Ezekiel) was not very appropriate, and the students were not particularly keen on doing this. As soon as it became clear that other subject staff were in need of more teaching time, I offered to surrender these Fifth Form lessons to enable me to teach Modern Languages. In addition, I was expected to complete with Upper Sixth students a subject course created by my predecessor Rev Alan Charters and known as "Plesionics". This was derived from the Greek word 'Plesion', meaning 'Neighbour'. It was a study of the major issues faced by the world's developing nations, mainly in Africa. The subject was validated as equivalent to an 'A' level subject by Sussex University. After frantic reading and struggling to get to grips with the course I brought it to an end after one year. As a result, I then had more spare lessons on my timetable which I was able to offer to the Modern Languages Department. They seemed pleased to have me join them, regularly teaching German to 'O' level and occasionally teaching a little conversational French. Results in both Divinity and German were very pleasing indeed throughout my time at the College. By keeping careful notes of what I taught in each and every lesson I was able to ensure that the next lesson with any particular group always began with a few minutes revising what had been taught in the previous session. In German lessons I combined a very conversational and repetitive approach with instilling a firm grammatical understanding.

As Chaplain I led College Assemblies on most days, and once each week at the Lower School. I prepared boys, mostly Boarders (as well as some Ladies' College Boarders) for Confirmation and presented candidates annually to the Bishop. I also served as the Bishop's Chaplain when he came to conduct the Confirmation Services for the College. I regularly accompanied the Director of Music and the College choir on their annual visits to St. Malo during the Week of Prayer for Christian Unity. There the boys sang at Mass in the Cathedral and at various other Catholic Churches in the area. On these visits I was usually invited by Père Michel Leutellier to read the Gospel and sometimes to concelebrate with the Catholic Priests at the Mass. This was particularly frowned upon by Catholic Priests in Guernsey when they got to hear about it. It also astonished Guernsey's Anglican and Methodist clergy, for such a concelebration at Holy Communion between Anglicans and Methodists could normally never take place, let alone between Catholics and Methodists. On one occasion I was asked at twelve hours' notice to preach in French in Dol Cathedral in the presence of the Cardinal Archbishop of Rennes. This entailed much burning of the midnight oil!

From my point of view, my position as an ordained Methodist Minister serving as Chaplain of a School that was of an Anglican foundation worked very well. On a biennial basis I was enabled and encouraged to attend the Anglican Chaplains' Conference held each time in a different one of the most famous boys' Public Schools. At these events I was probably the only Chaplain present who did not have a Public-School background, whereas many of those present knew each other well from school days.

I led Sunday worship, called 'House Prayers', in the College Hall for the boarders and a few members of staff and occasional visitors, including the Principal and the few boarders from the Ladies College. The service lasted around 35 to 40 minutes. The Bishop of Winchester was happy with the arrangement that once a month this service took the form of a service of Holy Communion, so long as I conducted it using the Methodist rite. In my own mind there was and is no difference between the Anglican and the Methodist rites in any case. I was very slow in appreciating however what a disadvantage it probably was to the Anglican Deanery on the Island that I was not one of their own. It meant they were not free to use me as a stand-in Priest for them, particularly in celebrating the Eucharist, in cases of clergy illness, forced absence, priests' holidays and interregna etc. It therefore came as quite a surprise when I realized that I would be made very welcome if I were in fact to become an Anglican; and I was alerted to this possibility in October 1974. I had noticed at one evening service at Les Camps Methodist Church in St Martin's that the Dean was sitting in the congregation. He was also Chairman of the College Board of Directors. Shortly afterwards I received an unexpected letter couched in Biblical references implying that perhaps the time might be right for me to consider making a major change of direction of some kind. There were three main reasons why I replied rejecting the idea of becoming an Anglican priest, for I guessed that that was what was being hinted at.

Firstly, I would be revoking a lifelong vow that I made at my Ordination at the Methodist Conference in Preston in 1963. Secondly, I felt certain that it would harm ecumenical relations on the Island and possibly further afield; folk would regard it as clear evidence that ecumenical cooperation and sharing did not really work. Thirdly, the requirement that I should be re-ordained in order to become an Anglican Priest would imply that I regarded my ordination and the ordination of all Methodist Ministers past, present and future as invalid, incomplete or inadequate.

ONLY JUST

(Just as the Roman Catholic Church considers the Church of England at the Reformation to have lost the direct line of succession of Bishops' ordination going right back to St Peter, who was called "The Rock" on whom Christ stated he would build his Church, so too the Church of England officially still regards Methodism as having lost its line of continuity from the Church of England (because Methodism ordains its own Ministers). John Wesley, the founder of Methodism, was a committed Priest of the Church of England all his life, but he found it necessary in 1784 to 'set apart', 'appoint' or 'ordain' three men to go as priests to America. During the American War of Independence, as British troupes withdrew, the Church of England lost interest in America, leaving over 15,000 Anglicans (who had been enthused in the practice of their faith by Wesley's Methodist principles) with no opportunity to receive Holy Communion. Having failed to persuade the Bishop of London to ordain priests for America, he very reluctantly took it upon himself to do so. Thus began the rift which even the great scheme of 1971 (known as "The Conversation"), planned to reunite our two Churches, sadly failed to heal.)

Methodists have come to believe that when Jesus told St Peter 'You are Peter, and upon this rock I will build my Church" he was making something of a pun on the word 'Petros' and referring to the 'rock'-like quality of the faith that Peter had just confessed by recognizing Jesus as the Messiah.

Looking back, over fifty years later, in retirement, despite now preferring the formality and order of Anglican worship and the Church of England's choral heritage and the pattern of receiving the Eucharist on a regular weekly basis, I feel that I nonetheless made the right decision to remain faithful to my Methodist calling. Being a Methodist was really an accident of my birth and upbringing. Had I been brought up and confirmed as a Member of the Church of England and ordained into the Anglican Priesthood I would have been equally happy but could well have remained as College Chaplain for a further fifteen years until retirement. However, I was ready for a fresh challenge. Having said that, I tend to feel that the Methodist authorities in the Channel Islands never fully understood or valued my presence as an ordained Minister working outside of their control within an Independent College and later in Guernsey's Education system. I was given no service of induction, installation or welcome in 1971; the Methodist Church locally never actually used me in any educating capacity within their work in the Channel Islands and made no acknowledgement of my retirement from Education in 1995, of 50 or 60 years as an Ordained Minister in 2013 and 2023, or of 50 years of leading Methodist acts of worship on the Island in 2021. This would probably not have been the case had I been ordained Priest in the Church of England, where I feel that the local community is regarded more clearly as the realm to which God's Kingdom relates. *The Kingdom of God is surely wherever God rules and wherever His will is done. The Church is not the Kingdom of God; it exists to be an agent of that Kingdom.*

One tragic aspect of College life at that time was the fact that during my 9 years as Chaplain no less than 9 boys lost their lives, mostly as a result of motoring accidents. I conducted some of their funerals which were held in Anglican Churches.

Life was extremely busy during term time. College functioned on five and a half days per week, and in addition I was required to lead the Sunday morning service for the Boarders. Lesson preparation, marking, fortnightly assessments, Parents' Evenings and the writing of countless reports filled my evenings and weekends. One of the main pressures was that of always having to keep one step ahead of the very bright, of whom there were many. I was also expected to take the Under 14's Hockey Team and was in charge of the Social Service Unit for any boys who were neither in the Officers' Training Corps nor following the Duke of Edinburgh scheme. The amount of lesson preparation and other paperwork was extensive, and I was generally still working very late every night including at weekends. After 6 years, in 1977, the Principal, Richard Wheadon, invited me to add to my duties the position of Housemaster of Country House, and this additional responsibility involved a lot more counselling and liaising with parents. I held this position for 3 years until I left the College in 1980. I had had a verbal gentlemen's agreement with Mr. Day that I should aim at serving the College for around 10 years.

During the 1970's there had been sharp inflation which led to teachers' salaries being raised. This encouraged us to consider moving house, which we did in 1979. We sold Maison des Ruettes in Bailiff's Cross Road for £16,500 (having bought it eight years earlier for £6,850, and we moved to the Farmhouse in Rue du Catillon at St Peter's, for which we paid £25,000. We remained there only four years, largely because it involved so much travelling for all five of us. At one stage we were having to travel daily to five different schools. However, while we were there, we experienced a house fire. It began in the kitchen and was caused by a chip pan of fat igniting whilst we were out. It resulted in Wendy having to cook in the garage, the children to camp on the lawn, whilst Wendy and I relied on the kindness of our neighbour Diana Hooker (formerly Curle). Our Insurance Company's appointed loss adjuster ensured that the repairs and redecoration costs were kept to a minimum, but we were unaware that if we had appointed a loss adjuster for ourselves, we would all have been able to live in comfort at a hotel until the renovations were competed.

St Peter Port School

In 1980, after nine very demanding and fulfilling years, I applied for a position in the States Sector of Education on the Island. It was in that year that the Methodist Church was seeking to encourage the Church to consider its mission alongside those less fortunate in society. This initiative was called 'Mission alongside the Poor". That was also the year in which GCSE replaced GCE 'O' level exams. This immediately required a doubling of the teaching time for subjects such as Divinity because of the introduction of coursework. It was not something that I would have happily become involved in, for I would no longer have been able to get to know all the Boys at the College as a result of teaching them at some time or other. Furthermore, it would have meant that I would probably have had to withdraw from teaching Modern Languages, which I enjoyed. It had also meant that my teaching had a strengthened sense of authority, which had a spin-off in that in the eyes of students Divinity seemed to gain respect. I therefore applied for a Post as Deputy Headteacher of St. Peter Port Secondary School and, against four other candidates being interviewed, somewhat to my surprise, I was appointed. The School had been opened in 1968 by H.R.H. Princess Alexandra, with Mr Charles Tiller as its first Headmaster, he having moved with his pupils from what previously had been the Vauvert Secondary Modern School. On having a heart attack, he was soon succeeded in 1971 by John Whight.

ONLY JUST

For me this move in 1980 proved to be quite a culture shock. Within a few months of my arrival Mr Whight had a nervous breakdown and I became Acting Headmaster, later to be appointed Head. During my first week as Headmaster our Head Girl Amanda Le Marquand was tragically killed in a motoring accident near Rocque Balan in the Vale and I conducted her funeral service at St Stephen's Church. The main stresses at St Peter Port School came from the very different ethos for teaching and learning and from a certain amount of very challenging behaviour from a small minority of pupils, particularly in the third and fourth forms (now called Years 9 & 10). Many arrived at 11 with low self-esteem and from broken homes, having recently been deemed to be failures following the 11+ examination. Often their parents had low expectations of their children, and some parents recalled themselves having had an unpleasant experience of education at the School. There was certainly less rigour in the teaching and learning, lower academic expectation, and it was expected that discipline would be maintained by the use of corporal punishment.

Within a few months of my arrival the Headmaster, Mr. John Whight, tragically, following the death of his daughter in a road accident in the Queen's Road, had a nervous breakdown and I was immediately required to become Acting Head. After about 8 months of illness, he retired on health grounds. When his position was advertised, I applied, and again, against four other candidates, was successful at interview. The position of Headteacher in this School had apparently also taken its toll on Mr. Whight's two predecessors. Mr. Stutchbury had died whilst in office at Vauvert, and Mr. Tiller had retired early following a heart attack, brought on, so they say, when a girl stood up to him and told him what he could do with himself. The position was undoubtedly very stressful. My two successors also retired early: one with high blood pressure and the next on the grounds of ill health. The mother of one persistent miscreant once encountered me in the park whilst out walking and poking me in the chest, told me in no uncertain terms that I only survived "because of your God", which I found quite shocking, yet very humbling.

In 1983 we decided we should move house to be in town. We therefore sold the Farmhouse for £65,000. With a profit of £20,000 we were able to do three important things. Firstly, we made some alterations necessary at our new home (Almorah, in Mont Arrive, St Peter Port for which we paid £45,000), secondly it enabled us to send Carys at the age of 16 to the Purcell School in London for her Sixth Form education. Thirdly, to our extreme good fortune, we were enabled (thanks to an oversight on the part of the Guernsey Sates some years earlier) to 'buy in' 16 and 12 back years of pension rights, ensuring that on retirement we would both receive pensions equivalent to having served in the teaching profession for 40 years.

Changes in society during the following years were inevitably reflected in the life of the School and its pupils. These changes included aspects of the information revolution that were taking place, the increased pressure on young people to gain exam qualifications, the general questioning of authority (requiring a very different style of management), the demand for increased accountability on the part of those in authority and a growing disintegration of family life.

The first major problem arose in the staff room, where certain long serving members of staff regarded their sole function and responsibility to be to teach their own particular subject. Personal, Social and Health Education (PSHE) was being introduced at that time, and some Staff members at first regarded this as an attempt at social engineering. Gradually these older members of staff came to realize that education was changing and that the school could no longer be regarded as existing for the convenience of the Staff, but rather for the benefit of the pupils, who were there not simply to be taught certain academic subjects, but to be educated for life.

The next major change concerned the matter of discipline. In 1981, very soon after my appointment as Head, corporal punishment was fortunately at last abolished in Guernsey Schools. Mr. Tiller (who had retired early) allegedly walked around the school with the cane tucked inside his sock and was known to use it frequently and publicly. Mr. Whight had also made fairly frequent use of this form of punishment. In my early weeks I managed to eliminate it entirely. With its welcome abolition however, the whole approach to handling issues of bullying, abuse and indiscipline had to alter. Already within society in general there had been growing for some time a tendency, increasingly on the part of adults, to challenge authority. No longer would a youngster receive further punishment at home when a parent learned that the child had been disciplined for misbehaving in school. In place of the threat of a short, sharp shock at school, schools had to put in place new structures for controlling behaviour and a fresh approach to classroom discipline. Codes of conduct had to be discussed and negotiated with every year group, so that offenders could justifiably be reminded of what their peers had agreed were the fair rules. Consultation and counselling had to be greatly increased, with the involvement of parents and others. This was very, very time-consuming. Referral of pupils to the Educational

Psychologist or Psychiatrist, with lengthy reports (including Court Reports), became necessary. This inevitably took time and throughout the 15 years that I was at the School I unfortunately tended to get to know better those who behaved badly rather than the many good students. Staff also had to undergo in-service training to enable them to acquire the difficult skills required to deal with challenging behaviour in their classes. The special needs department had to be expanded to contain not only a unit for those with learning problems, but also a unit for pupils with emotional and behavioural difficulties.

The Inservice Training of the Staff became increasingly important during the years from 1980 to 1995. This was because of the numerous changes taking place. There was the phasing out of the Certificate of Secondary Education and of G.C.E.'O' level exams, which resulted in pupils in all schools, whether non-selective, selective or private, being expected to sit the same GCSE exams. The introduction of the National Curriculum, for which by this time Wendy was in charge in Guernsey as Primary Education Officer at the Education Department, also took place in the early 1990's. Guernsey's own approach to this had to be devised and introduced, and for this much re-training of staff was involved. A system of school self-appraisal (externally validated by HMI Inspectors) was introduced to replace the old School Inspections. More paperwork was inevitable. Handling the school budget, producing the school timetable and dealing with a reduction in staff numbers (due to a decrease in the birth rate) caused considerable problems. To the dismay of certain pupils some important minority subjects, such as music, were squeezed out of the curriculum to the further disadvantage of some students. Teaching styles and subject content had to change.

At the same time there was a big upsurge in the introduction of new technological equipment. When I was appointed in 1980 the school had only four telephone lines, one to the Office (with extensions to the Staff Room and to the Head's and Deputy-Head's Study and one to the P.E./Games Department in case of accidents or emergencies). There were no mobile phones, no televisions, no computers, no fax machines, no white boards, no internet. By 1995 there was a phone, a television and at least one computer in every classroom. The playing fields, which were constantly waterlogged in Winter, were eventually given a herring-bone drainage system in 1988; and, for the school's 21st birthday in 1989, we were honoured with a return visit by H.R.H. the Princess Alexandra, and tennis courts and a hard surface playing area were built.

Pre-Vocational courses were introduced in 1982. These proved to be very successful. They were the idea of my Deputy-Head, John Loaring, who had had experience of such courses in B.A.O.R. Schools in Germany. They were validated by the City and Guilds. The same year saw the establishment of a strong Parent/Teacher Association which worked tirelessly for the benefit of the School. In particular, the Association helped to raise sufficient funds over ten years for us to build an outdoor swimming pool. It was opened in 1995 as the 'John Loaring Memorial Pool' by his Guernsey-born brother Richard Loaring (who lived in South Africa and was regarded as their 'Cliff Richard'). We were required to hand the pool over to the States Education Authority, who sadly stopped maintaining it after a few years, and I last saw it abandoned and filled with discarded furniture.

With the demise of CSE exams and the introduction of GCSE for all schools in 1986, at first the results were extremely disheartening, for the pupils' results could immediately be compared with those of the students who at 11 had been selected for the Grammar School or the Colleges; but gradually courses were selected, such as Drama and Combined Sciences, which were better suited to the needs of the young people and in which they achieved greater success. The introduction of the National Curriculum in 1993 brought about the need for the re-training of all Staff. It required staff to question and evaluate everything that they had hitherto been teaching, as well as their methodology. In the same year the number of St Peter Port School pupils to achieve the Gold standard of the Duke of Edinburgh's Award Scheme reached thirty. This was marked by an invitation from Prince Philip for Hazel Crawley, who had led the students to achieve their gold awards, and me, to attend a reception at Buckingham Palace.

Bomb Scare

Life was not without its crises and stresses. On one particular Friday afternoon whilst external exams were in progress in the Hall I received a phone call from the Police informing me that they had received a call indicating that a bomb had been planted in the School, and that I should evacuate the building. I held my breath and took no action. A few minutes later the Police arrived. I explained that on the two previous Fridays there had been similar unfounded bomb scares which had caused disruption when the school had been evacuated, and that I did not want to interrupt the exams that were in progress on this particular occasion. It was also raining heavily. "Be it on your head", were the words of the Police Officer that still occasionally haunt my dreams. I asked him to sit with me in my study for twenty-five minutes until the external examination was finished, when I would ring the bell to dismiss the rest of the school a few minutes early. They were probably the longest twenty-five minutes of my life; heat was rising as my pulse was racing. A big risk. I survived, but only just. The upshot was that the following Friday police were sent to hide close to every public phone box in St Peter Port, and the truanting pupil was caught and subsequently appeared before the Juvenile Court.

Exam Scare

Another stressful time was on a Liberation Day (May 9th) in the 1980's. I spent the day on the telephone talking to a National Association of Headteachers lawyer in London about something that had happened the day before. Students had come out laughing from a GCSE Maths exam. My Deputy had asked them, "why the merriment?" "It was easy; we'd seen the questions before," came the reply. The Head of the Maths Department at the time happened also to be on the Panel responsible for moderating the questions. He had brought the questions home from London from the moderation meeting to work on them, but the plane that he was due to travel back on to the Mainland had been fogbound. He had therefore not returned the question papers. He had kept them and could not resist giving his struggling students some assistance. I therefore had to suspend him; whereupon he contacted his Union's lawyer to assist and defend him. I needed guidance and similar protection from the law. The end result was that the offending member of staff was given early retirement by the Education Council, and with enhancement, following medical pleading that his misdemeanor was caused by stress. The reaction of the rest of the staff was inevitably very cynical. The pupils were made to repeat the exam, much to their detriment; and the parents were greatly displeased.

ONLY JUST

Loss of staff

In 1980 the School had its largest intake of pupils from the Primary Schools (146), which meant that some very bright pupils arrived who, in a normal year might well have been selected for the Grammar School or one of the Colleges. When extra staff were required, the Head simply had to ask the Deputy Director of Education for more. Finding the staff, however, was seldom easy. Posts could only be advertised on the Mainland if no teachers with appropriate qualifications could be found locally. Occasionally we were obliged to accept staff that were surplus to the requirements of other Island Secondary Schools, particularly when their numbers on roll were decreasing. Very different skills were required of Staff at St Peter Port School, for some of the pupils, especially some with emotional and behavioural problems, needed very careful and individual attention. It became very difficult to recruit teachers from the Mainland, for the prospect of teaching pupils in a Secondary Modern School, and only to the then compulsory age of 15 did not appeal to most members of the profession, since they had grown accustomed to Comprehensive Education with the chance also to teach 'A' level students to the age of 18. Furthermore, during my fifteen years at the School we lost well over twenty of our most able members of staff by their obtaining positions either at the Grammar School or one of the Colleges. One could not blame them for wanting to move. Working in one of these other establishments would prove emotionally less stressful, more rewarding and they might also have the opportunity to rise higher on the teachers' pay scales.

One member of Staff we were particularly sad to lose was a recently appointed Deputy-Head. He had been appointed from the Mainland to replace the inspirational John Loaring, who had sadly died of cancer, and whose funeral I had conducted at St Stephen's Church. In the first three weeks at the School John's successor had made a very good impression with pupils and staff alike. He had led some excellent in-service training for us as well as for other Island schools. Then I received an unexpected telephone call from the Director of Education, Mike Hutchings, informing me that the Police would be arriving within fifteen minutes and that it would be unlikely that my Deputy-Head would be returning. Apparently, the Director had received a call from a Headmistress in England, asking if this certain gentleman was teaching on the Island and enquiring as to who had written his references. He looked up the appropriate file and was able to remind her that indeed she had written one of them, - a fact that she denied. It transpired that he had written his own glowing references. The police took him away in the 'Black Mariah' and we never saw him again.

Throughout my time at the School, as well as during the nine years at the College, I placed very great importance on School Assemblies and also played a part in writing the Island Guidelines for Collective Worship in all Island Schools. Assemblies were something to which I gave a lot of time in preparation as I regarded them as an important opportunity to put forward Christian values, and I usually based them on some recent topic of news or by talking about the remarkable achievements of role models in the fields of sport, medicine, science or discovery.

I took my turn as Chairman of the Guernsey Association of Headteachers and also served many years on the Island Apprenticeship Committee and the Island's Religious Education Advisory Committee, for which we produced a new syllabus.

 I was also asked to take on the position of Chairman of the Guernsey Branch of the NSPCC, which I held for 9 years, and to stand for election as a Douzainier for St. Peter Port, where I served for six years. It was at one of the Annual Meetings of the NSPCC that the President, Sir Charles Frossard endorsed Jurat Len Moss's suggestion that I should be encouraged to stand for election to become a Jurat of the Royal Court. A few years later when Sir Charles retired as NSPCC President on the Island, I was chosen to replace him. Unfortunately, soon afterwards the local Branch, which had a large band of helpers and house-to-house collectors, closed down. This was because Head Office in London decided to withdraw from the Island our NSPCC Child Protection Officer and to close the Family Support Centre in Fountain Street that had been opened by Princess Margaret. At the same time, they opened up a large Centre in Jersey where a very large child abuse investigation was underway. Our local support swiftly and understandably evaporated, for there would no longer be any NSPCC presence in our Bailiwick.

Throughout my time as Headmaster, I continued to offer about twenty or thirty Sunday mornings each year when the Methodist Church could plan to use my services leading worship and preaching in any of the many Methodist Churches in the Bailiwick. In 1971 there had been 28 Churches, divided into two Circuits (one English-speaking and one supposedly 'French'-speaking) . Within the 'French Circuit' one often heard the Guernsey Patois spoken, and congregations were always pleased when one chose at least one French hymn. In 2023, at time of writing, there are ten remaining Methodist Churches, in just one united Circuit (one being in Alderney and one in Sark), and I believe it would be more appropriate if there were just three or four. With so many remaining open and so few Methodist Ministers and Local Preachers available I feel some of the worship is not of the standard one had come to expect.

Occasionally other Churches would invite me to lead worship, including the Church of England, the Church of Scotland, the United Reformed Church, the Baptist Church and the Salvation Army. One invitation came from the Dean, the Very Rev'd Jeffery Fenwick which resulted in my preaching at the main Liberation Day Service in the Town Church on May 9th, 1992.

7 JURÉ JUSTICIER DE LA COURT ROYALE

ELECTION AS JURAT

Upon retirement from Education in 1995 on reaching the age of 60 I was asked to assist the Methodist Church in some way, having in mind that Methodist Ministers normally retire at 65. I therefore took on the voluntary role of Synod Secretary for the Channel Islands District and increased the number of preaching appointments that I offered each quarter to the Guernsey Circuit. However, in 1996, on the suggestion of the Senior Jurat Len Moss and of the Bailiff Sir Charles Frossard I was nominated and seconded by Deputy Tony Bran and Douzainier Michael Dene to stand for election by the States of Election as a Jurat of the Royal Court, but I was defeated by David Jorey. In 1998 I stood again and scraped in, but 'only just', by a single vote. Once sworn in, one was not allowed to retire for at least five years but was expected to serve to the age of seventy-five unless one's fellow eleven Jurats, by secret annual ballot when one reached the age of seventy, decided that one should not continue. Thus began, at my swearing in on St. Peter's Day 1998, twelve years of service as one of the twelve Jurats of the Royal Court, Jurés Justiciers de la Cour Royale, a title one is required to carry for the rest of one's life.

There was one most unfortunate consequence which came to light soon after my swearing in. For several years since her retirement from the position of Senior Education Officer for the States of Guernsey, with special responsibility for Primary Education and the introduction of the National Curriculum on the Island, Wendy had served as a member of the Island's States Prison Parole Board, helping to determine if and when it might be appropriate for a prisoner to be released early from their incarceration. The Bailiff, Sir de Vic Carey, on learning of her position on the Board, ruled that it was inappropriate for one member of a family to be sending criminals to prison for a set length of time whilst another had the power to share in the decision whether or not to release them early on parole. The upshot was that it was Wendy who sadly was caused to relinquish her position of responsibility in which she was giving valuable service to the Island, and which she knew was worthwhile.

This is but one of the countless sacrifices that Wendy made in order to make it possible for me to pursue my calling and to seize opportunities. For ten years as Minister of Methodist Churches in Stonehouse, Stafford and Abingdon we lived in what can only be described as genteel poverty, and Wendy skimped and saved and denied herself of the beautiful wardrobe and personal luxuries she deserved, in order, by scheming and invention to provide us with wonderful, wholesome meals and a healthy, balanced diet. In those days Ministers were expected to try and visit all Church members and adherents as frequently as possible, and one lived constantly with a sense of guilt for failing to achieve as much as one felt one should. With Wendy supporting me, it meant that it was she who carried the huge burden of housework, cooking, laundry, looking after our three children, as well as supporting me in the Church by teaching in the Sunday School, running the successful Toddlers' Club and leading the flourishing Young Wives Group. In addition, as soon as it became possible, she returned to teaching in order to help us make ends meet. Even whilst doing all this and carrying these responsibilities, with her wonderfully friendly and gregarious nature she welcomed and got to know all church members and shared their joys and sorrows. This was a huge help throughout my ministry, for I am, I think, more shy and reticent by nature.

Our move to Guernsey in 1971 required us to take out our first mortgage. This required Wendy to work full-time, first as Deputy-Head at Vauvert Infant School, then as Warden of the Teachers Centre and finally as a Senior Education Officer at the Education Department. With my roles as Chaplain and Housemaster at the College, then as Headmaster and finally as a Jurat, meant that Wendy again carried the major burdens of running the home and caring for the children's welfare.

By law, on my 75th birthday, my role as a Jurat came to an end in 2010. I count it as a great honour to have followed in the footsteps of the only other member of the Clergy (likewise a Methodist Minister) ever to serve as a Jurat of the Royal Court, namely the much-revered Jurat Rev. Sir John Leale. (He also spoke German.) John Leale was Knighted by the King for his services as President of the Controlling Committee during the Nazi Occupation of Guernsey. I was also only about the second or possibly third non-Guernsey man ever to be thus elected.

Role of Jurats

Jurats of the Royal Court in Guernsey have existed for nigh on 800 years, and all who have served since 1298 have their names recorded on the boards in the Jurats' Chambers. Jurats form the permanent, elected jury, administering justice in both criminal and civil trials. Unlike juries on the Mainland, whilst they are judges of fact, in criminal cases, Guernsey's Jurats determine not only the verdict in both criminal and civil matters, but also what sentence should be imposed in criminal cases and what damages should be awarded in civil matters. I soon learnt that in criminal matters our judgments had to be made on the basis of 'beyond reasonable doubt', whereas in civil matters they should be based 'on the law of probabilities'. The Judge would, at the conclusion of every trial, indicate to us the parameters within which we had to work when determining the sentence for any particular crime. He would also draw our attention to precedents when helping us to determine our judgements, always allowing us to take into account aggravating or mitigating factors.

It meant that for nine months of the year it was impossible to take a holiday and it placed great demands on both me and Wendy. However, we were able from time to time to escape briefly to our second home in Langrolay-sur-Rance (between Dinard and Dinan) that we had purchased on a whim on a rainy day soon after my mother's death in 1996.

Most of the criminal cases coming before the court were related to drug importations; but those who were sentenced were usually simply the "mules" and seldom if ever the major dealers. One felt sorry for these vulnerable people, but nonetheless, to protect the local population the laws in force on the Island were severe, because it was considered important to issue sentences that might protect the local population by attempting to reduce these illegal importations. This however tended to drive up the price of drugs on the street, thus making it even more enticing for big dealers to trap desperate young people into bringing these illicit goods into the Island.

During my 12 years on the Bench, we had four guilty murder trials, and I was called to sit on three of them (two involving former pupils of mine). I found it particularly horrendous having to spend several days studying dozens of dreadful pictures of victims and of the crime scenes.

In pairs we were frequently involved in visiting homes and hospitals to witness people's wills; individually we occasionally spent three cold hours in the vaults of Frossard House destroying hundreds of thousands of soiled bank notes (with the assistance of two civil servants); and from time to time, we were taken on a 'vue de justice' to help us judge the claims of appellants appealing against decisions of the Planning Authority. In groups of five, twice a week, we sat in the Conveyancing (or Contracts) Court approving the sale and purchase of property (real estate), witnessing other contracts and granting occasional liquor licenses.

The decisions we were called upon to make were inevitably often life-changing for the people that appeared before us. The twelve Jurats brought wide experience to the Bench from many walks of life, which enriched and informed our lengthy and demanding deliberations; and the camaraderie was both enjoyable and rewarding.

Jurats of the Royal Court are judges of fact. In criminal trials they determine not only the verdict (guilty or not guilty), as do juries on the Mainland, but also, with legal guidance from the presiding Judge, the appropriate sentence that it to be imposed following a guilty verdict. Historically there have always been 12 Jurats, but in 2008 a new law was passed by the Island Parliament (The States of Deliberation) which increased their number to 16. This change was felt to be necessary partly because of the increasing workload, but also in case there should ever be the need for a re-trial. Thus, criminal trials, following this change in 2008, are held with a jury of 8, thereby keeping a remaining eight in reserve.

It is said that election as a Jurat is the highest honour that Guernsey has in its power to confer on a resident of the Island, and that opinion tends to accord with that of the community as a whole. The role is, however, very demanding; all the more so when there were only twelve of us on the Bench.

History.

The first recorded mention of Jurats of the Royal Court was in the year 1179. The names of all Jurats elected since the year 1299 are known and are recorded on a Roll of Honour in the Jurats' Room in the Royal Court building. The 1441 'Précepte d'Assise' states that the Jurats must be "the most notable, impartial, wise, loyal and rich of the Island"! Until 1607, Jurats were elected by all the male property owners, and these elections were held in each parish on Sundays after Church; but in 1607 the States of Election was established by King James 1st. This States of Election still exists and consists of 100 people: These are the Bailiff, the existing Jurats, the Church of England Rectors, the elected States Deputies, and representatives of the 10 Island Douzaines. There are a number of historical cases where individuals refused to serve, proved to be dishonest, or accepted bribes; such men were dispatched to London and imprisoned in the Tower of London. Originally a Jurat was elected for the duration of his life. He could not retire, except on the ground of ill health. In the 19th century several Jurats sought the permission of the Sovereign to retire but were refused. Until 2008, Jurats served until the age of 70, or, on the judgement of their fellow Jurats, their service could be extended annually until they reached the age of 75. Most therefore retired at 75, as did I. Since 2008 however, the tenure of office of a Jurat cannot be extended beyond the age of 72.

Until comparatively recently it was only men that could be nominated for the position of Jurat. Catholics, atheists, brewers and women were never allowed to stand for election. With regard to all these categories the law was changed in 1950. Thus, in 1985 the first woman was elected.

The Various Duties of Jurats

Criminal Trials. Each criminal trial now starts with eight Jurats. The law requires a minimum of seven. Decisions are reached by a simple majority, but to determine that a person is guilty of an offense the Jurats have to be certain of the individual's guilt "beyond reasonable doubt." If they judge the person to be guilty, they are then, at a later gathering of the Court, required to decide the sentence that will be imposed. In this task they are guided by the Judge regarding precedents and the parameters that the law allows, but the final decision is with the Jurats.

Civil Trials. Each Civil case requires three or four Jurats to sit with a Judge. Their decision has to be made on the balance of probabilities, and after it is announced, they are required to issue a reasoned judgement explaining how they arrived at that decision. These cases can be very long, maybe lasting up to eight weeks or longer. All judgements, both in criminal as well as civil cases, can be appealed against, and three High Court Judges from the Mainland visit the Island three times each year to consider any such appeals.

Full Court duties. Twelve Jurats sit as a Full Court once a month. They may be required to consider appeals against decisions made by certain States Departments or Courts in Alderney and Sark. They regularly have to agree to place on the Statute Book any new legislation made by the Island Parliament (the States of Deliberation) after it has received royal assent from the Queen's Privy Council. Another function of the Full Court is to "swear in" new officials, e.g. A new Lieutenant Governor, a new Bailiff or Deputy Bailiff, Lieutenant-Bailiffs, new Appeal Court Judges, new Jurats, Advocates (Lawyers), Doctors, etc. They also have to listen to reports on safety issues relating to the airport, the harbours, local quarries, bakeries and the storage of explosives and fireworks.

Ordinary Court duties. Three or four Jurats have to sit twice a month to consider applications from people wishing to hold liquor licences and to examine plans for any proposed alterations to licensed premises. They have to approve the appointment of official guardians and family councils, the swearing in of States Deputies, Douzainiers and other Parish Officials. They have to consider applications from companies to change their name or to go into liquidation or into administration. They have to consider any applications to evict tenants for non-payment of rent or for failing to keep the terms of a contract. They swear in liquidators, give final approval to child adoptions, and also to foreign nationals seeking naturalisation as British Citizens in the Bailiwick.

Private Court duties

Conveyancing Court duties. Twice each week 5 Jurats have to sit in the Conveyancing Court to witness contracts being agreed and to witness the sale or purchase of real estate. They also authorise the issuing of occasional liquor licences and licences to anyone wishing to set up as a street trader.

Individual duties. Occasionally a Jurat is required to be appointed as a "Commissioner", to call and preside at a meeting of Creditors when a Company goes "en desastre" or into liquidation. The purpose of this is to agree to the allocation of residual assets in accordance with the law. Each Jurat is also required occasionally to superintend the destruction of bank notes, when every bank note has to pass through the Jurat's hands onto the shredding machine, and he or she has to verify the total number of notes destroyed and their value. (I think that upon my retirement in 2010 I held the record of 160,000 notes being destroyed in the 3 hours allotted).

Ceremonial Occasions. Jurats are expected to attend important ceremonies on Liberation Day, on Remembrance Sunday and at 'Chief Pleas' (the start of the Legal Year), and also whenever a Lieutenant Governor or Bailiff or Deputy Bailiff retires and when new ones are sworn in and take up office. They are also usually summoned to appear fully robed on the occasion of any official visit by a member of the Royal Family.

ONLY JUST

A few cases I well recall

A Bank Closure in 2008

Jurats are asked to give their assent to the swearing in of a new Lieutenant Governor, a new Bailiff or Judge, of Crown Officers, Lawyers, Doctors, Liquidators, newly Elected Jurats, States Deputies, Parish Officials etc. We are required to approve the opening and closure of any banks, finance companies, bakeries, firearms vendors, officials licensed to sell alcohol, family councils, alterations to licensed premises etc.

Each October, at the start of the legal year all Jurats process to the Town Church for the annual Chief Pleas Service. The same evening, they are invited to a very generous meal. It is thought that the Sovereign pays for it.

During the meal held at the Duke of Richmond Hotel in October 2008, at about 9.30 p.m., I was in the middle of eating my main course, when an official from the Royal Court unexpectedly tapped me on the shoulder. He explained that I and two other Jurats, being the Jurats of the Quarter, would immediately be required to sit at night for a Civil Case in the Royal Court starting at 10 o'clock. This was unprecedented in all the years I had been on the Bench. We left before the pudding and coffee were served. The three of us arrived at Court and robed. As usual we began with the Lord's Prayer spoken in French (with a Deputy Greffier using the Court's version which has for many years been recited inaccurately despite my request for it to be corrected: – *"....donne-nous notre pain quotidien et <u>nous pardonne</u> nos offenses..."*. which assumes that the good Lord forgives us our sins without our requesting it) It should of course be *"..... et pardonne-nous."*. Then we were told that we were to hear an application from a Bank to close its doors and to cease trading. The Bank in question was a branch of an Icelandic Bank. The three of us listened to all the evidence of insolvency. It was argued that the assets of the Bank were no longer sufficient to match the deposits of its clients. We came to the conclusion that if we did not accede to the request, there would be long queues outside the Bank the next morning. The rich would probably be at the front of the queue and the poor at the back. After lengthy deliberation we decided to put the Bank into administration, and we appointed a Liquidator to garner and distribute the assets (in the manner and priority as specified in the law). The matter was further complicated in that the Manager of the Guernsey Branch of the Bank was the son of the Senior Jurat at that time, which of course excluded him from being called upon to assist in judging the case. That is an experience I shall long remember.

A Civil Case of 1998

A cyclist who represented Guernsey in the British Commonwealth Games in November 1998, when he was 29, was cycling on a road in Guernsey, when he was struck by a car. He was not wearing a crash helmet. His injuries were very severe. He suffered brain damage and will need 24-hour care for the rest of his life. The driver of the car was found guilty of dangerous driving. His family made a claim for 20 million pounds from the car driver's Insurance Company. This claim was brought to the Royal Court in 2009. I was one of 3 Jurats who considered this very difficult case, which lasted over six weeks. The claim was for the highest sum of money ever claimed for personal damages in a British Court.

During the six weeks we had to make hundreds of decisions.

For the rest of his life, he would need 3 carers, each working for 8 hours a day, and a fourth carer for weekends and holidays. How long would he live? How much would the cost-of-living rise during his lifetime? What education or therapy would he require? Did he need a specially adapted home for his wheelchair? Should he be given a cycle track or a swimming pool in order to allow him to exercise? How much money should we grant him for annual holidays? What compensation should we grant him for a loss of his social life and for the fact that he could no longer earn his living as a taxi driver? What clothing would he need, and how long would his clothes last? We had to answer these and many other impossible questions. Experts from the Mainland came to plead and present arguments for and against our making generous judgements.

After six long weeks we reached a figure of £9,337,852.27. The family believed that this figure was too low, so they took the matter to Guernsey's Court of Appeal, which meets 3 times every year, when 3 High Court Judges from England visit the Island to consider such Appeals. They concluded that all our calculations were fair and just, apart from one, namely the estimated cost of future inflation. In England an award could be made whereby the appellant could be paid in instalments, but no such law exists in Guernsey. The Court of appeal therefore increased the award for damages to £14 million pounds. This was the highest amount ever awarded in any British Court for physical injury following an accident.

The car driver's Insurance Company appealed to Her Majesty's Privy Council in London, claiming that our original award of £9 million was correct; but the Privy Council endorsed the decision of the Court of Appeal: £14 million. We still see the former cyclist in town occasionally. At the time of writing he is 48 years of age.

Criminal Cases

The majority of criminal trials during my 12 years as a Jurat (1998-2010) involved the importation of or dealing in drugs. Guernsey is very strict regarding drugs, for it is the wish of our Parliament to protect our own population. Therefore, our Customs officials are constantly on the alert and our sentencing policy is very strict and rigid. The result, of course, is that because it is more difficult and more dangerous for drug dealers to import drugs, there are less drugs on the Island. Therefore, the price of drugs rises, and the dealers are all the more keen to succeed in their efforts to import drugs into the Island.

There were four murder trials during my 12 years as a Jurat. I was involved in three of these, two of which involved former pupils of the school where I was Headmaster from 1980-1995, so they were known to me. I could have recused myself from these and many other cases, but I did not.

If I recognised any person who appeared on any charge, I was always required to declare it at the start of the trial. Only once was I asked to leave the Bench, and that was at the request of a young man accused of rape, who was subsequently proved not guilty.

The Clameur de Haro

The Clameur is an ancient legal injunction of restraint used by a person who believes he or she is being wronged at that moment. It survives as a fully enforceable law to this day. It is used very infrequently for matters affecting land.

Based on Norman law, it is believed to be a plea to Rollo, the

10th century founder of the Duchy of Normandy. Originally the cry was probably Ha – Rollo, meaning "chase him".

The 'criant' must be on his knees before two witnesses in the presence of the wrong-doer, and in the location of the offense. The 'criant' puts his hand in the air and must call out "Haro, Haro, Haro. A l'aide, mon Prince. On me fait tort". Then he must say the Lord's Prayer in French. When he hears this the alleged wrongdoer must cease until the matter is adjudicated in court. If he fails to cease, he will be fined whether he is right or not. If the 'criant' has called "Haro....." without a valid reason, he will have to pay a penalty.

He then says the Lord's Prayer in French. The clamour then has to be lodged at the Greffe (Guernsey's Registry Office) within 24 hours.

One day in about 2003 I was sitting with four other Jurats in the Conveyancing (or Contract) Court. This Court is held every Tuesday and Thursday morning at 9.30 a.m. Three Jurats have to witness every contract that is agreed and the sale and purchase of every property. The room was crowded and very noisy. Suddenly it went silent. Obviously, people had been expecting something to happen, but we Jurats knew nothing. Through the crowd appeared a little man who seemed to have no legs. I thought to myself, "This poor man has no legs, and yet he is coming straight to my desk". Then he began, and I suddenly noticed that in fact he was on his knees. He shouted "Haro. Haro. Haro. A l'aide, mon Prince. On me fait tort" "Notre Père qui es aux cieux...." etc. He then asked me to witness his clamour, which I did. He then asked me to register it. At the time I had no idea what that meant, so I asked the senior Jurat, and he told me not to do it, but to send him to the Bailiff (since only the Bailiff could register it and adjudicate on the complaint). What he was objecting to was the fact that his wife was about to sell their home. But in fact, as we later discovered, the house belonged not to him, nor to them both, but solely to her. But that was a most unusual event. The Clameur is raised vary rarely, perhaps only once in 20 or 30 years, and seldom if ever within the precincts of the Royal Court.

Chief Pleas Service 2012

Two years after my retirement as Jurat I was invited by the Bailiff, Sir Richard Collas, to preach at the annual Chief Pleas Service held at the commencement of the new legal year, on October 1st, 2012. Sir Richard had still been a pupil in the third year of the Upper Sixth at Elizabeth College when I became Chaplain at the College in 1971. I took as my text, "Judge not, that ye be not judged."

Retirement from the Bench

On my seventy-fifth birthday in 2010 the law required me to retire from the Bench. Two years earlier we had moved from "Almorah" in Mont Arrive to Admiral Park's Vega Apartments, a property costing £365,000. We had paid £45,000 for Almorah in 1983, and in 2008 it fetched £615,000, and we chose to share part of the profit (£90,000) equally between our three children.

Throughout our first fifty years in Guernsey, I continued to conduct Methodist Church Services within the Bailiwick, and did so on well over a thousand occasions, but found it necessary to cease leading worship in 2021 due to the increasing effects of old age. In addition, I had often been invited to take Assemblies at schools other than my own and to preach in Churches of other denominations. One invitation came from my *alma mater,* the Crypt Grammar School, where I had been a pupil from 1943 to 1954, to preach at their annual Commemoration Service in Gloucester Cathedral. On eleven occasions I had sung in the choir at that annual service, but on this occasion, it was quite a strange and somewhat disconcerting experience; it was rather like being a 12-year-old pupil once again, as if a child of twelve among the spectators at a Test Match were suddenly pulled out of the crowd and told he was needed to open the batting for England. However, it must have gone reasonably well, for the Headmaster thanked me warmly and kindly asked for a copy of the sermon, which then appeared in full in the annual Crypt School magazine. It is reproduced later in this document.

My pastoral work continued well into retirement, for I continued to be asked to take services and to conduct the funerals of friends and others whom I had known well for many years. These included members of staff who had been colleagues of mine at Elizabeth College or at St Peter Port School, and the parents of several pupils whom I had taught, and sadly, several former pupils.

Two close friends in particular stand out in my memory because they were both members of the Town Church, namely Jenny Randall and Jane Rihoy (wife of John, owner of J W Rihoy and son). John had generously supported the charitable work of my brother Sebert in the Dominican Republic. At a time when there was a shortage of work for his employees John, at his firm's expense, had sent a group of craftsmen with his son Gavin to build "Guernsey Classrooms" for a school that Sebert had built in the village of Barahona where there had been no school. Jane, who was very ill, asked if I would take her and Jenny Randall Holy

Communion in Jenny's home. It was at a time when the Town Church was in Interregnum, so I asked the Vice Dean Mike Kearle if this would be in order, to which he readily agreed. Shortly afterwards Jenny, the widow of the former Town Church Treasurer Brian Randall, was receiving palliative care in the Hospice and she made a similar request, since the Dean and Rector had still not yet arrived. Jenny had served the Island as a midwife, and she greeted me as I arrived to give her Communion with the words, "Well, when mothers were in labour, I gave them gas and air, and here you are, bringing me Mass and prayer." I quoted this at her funeral, and it was a very emotional moment in what for me was a deeply moving service. I simply refer to these occasions because it shows how, in keeping with the teaching of Jesus, when human need so requires, man-made rules (in these cases regarding Episcopal ordination) can be ignored. *(If the same guideline had been followed when John Wesley begged the Bishop of London to ordain two priests to enable American Christians to receive Communion during the War of American Independence, Methodism would probably never have broken away from the Church of England.)*

ONLY JUST

8 LINKS WITH BIBERACH

One Committee on which I was pleased to serve was that of the Friends of Biberach Association. During the war-time occupation of Guernsey by Nazi forces Hitler ordered that, as a reprisal for the internment of German civilians in neutral Iran in the Summer of 1941, the families of any non-Guernsey born residents of the Island were to be deported to an internment camp in Southern Germany. As a result, 1,013 Guernsey residents with links with England were transported to Biberach-an-der-Riss, many at 24 hours' notice, in 1942 and 1943. After two or three years of severe deprivation the camp was liberated on 23rd April 1945.

In 1997 the Bailiff received from Oberbuergermeister Fettback (Mayor of Biberach) an invitation for former deportees to visit the town. It was his wish that a "Bridge of Reconciliation" be built between our two communities. It was in the same year that the Guernsey Council of Churches, under the Chairmanship of Mrs Rosemary Jagger, (daughter of Raymond Falla, who was responsible for obtaining food for the Island by travelling thousands of miles in occupied France during the war) responded to an appeal from the

European Council of Churches to focus Christians' attention to the need for reconciliation. As a result, I was sent as a delegate to represent the Island's Christian community at the Second European Ecumenical Assembly held in Graz, Austria. I went both as a delegate and also as a stallholder with the purpose of inviting particularly any interested German Christians to visit the Island for a 'Week of Reconciliation' in September 1997. One result was that I was invited to accompany a second group of former deportees as member of the Island clergy and as interpreter on a week's visit to Biberach. Another result was the formation of a "Friends of Biberach Association" of which I was appointed Vice-Chairman.

The theme of the Graz Assembly was "Reconciliation, Gift of God and Source of New Life". Over 20,000 Christians of all traditions from all over Europe attended. My task was twofold. Firstly, I was sent as a delegate to the conference of national Church representatives, and secondly, I tried singlehandedly to run a stall inviting attendees (in particular German Christians) to visit Guernsey for a week of reconciliation. Those who showed the greatest desire to travel were from the recently liberated East European countries, formerly part of the Soviet Union, but they were short of money to enable them to travel further. I was surprised at that Assembly to hear of recycling and conservation being regarded, particularly in parts of Germany, as an essential part of the mission of the Christian Church. This was important new thinking to me.

Guernsey's Week of Reconciliation in 1997 proved to be a considerable success. I was privileged to serve on the planning committee. The Chairman and Secretary (Rosemary Jagger and Frances Stanton) had succeeded in tracing the last

German to preach to the occupying forces in St Sampson's Church prior to Liberation Day 1945, namely Pastor Buerkert, aged 84. His description of tragic events in the Bailiwick, and particularly on Sark, were hair-raising and, emotionally, hard to repeat.

ONLY JUST

9 RETIREMENT

After relinquishing my seat on the Jurats' Bench in 2010, after twelve demanding yet fascinating years, I continued to take about twenty Methodist Church services each year until, at the age of 87, I found it necessary to stop preaching. Wendy often reminded me that when I was young and sitting in a congregation when an elderly man was leading the worship, I had often told her not to allow me to carry on doing so if I ever reached his age. Thus, my/our links with Methodism became more and more tenuous, for I joined Wendy on a regular basis in worshipping at the C of E Town Church, which I am pleased now to regard as my spiritual home. With more time and slower thinking I found one of Parkinson's Laws to be very true, namely, that the time to perform a task increases or decreases in proportion to the amount of time available. So, whereas sermon-writing had once been a Saturday evening task, with the reward for completing it being the opportunity to watch 'Match of the Day' on BBC television, it tended to take several days or even weeks working on and off to produce one sermon; for I was never satisfied that it was completed. I also began to find that I was starting to feel a bit confused in the pulpit, although kind members of the congregation assured me that it never appeared to be the case. Wendy had always attended the Town Church, supporting our three children as members of the choir, for years being in charge of the flower rota and welcoming countless visitors throughout the week. By joining her I found the more formal worship, the beautiful and well-chosen wording and the regular celebration of the Eucharist very conducive and rewarding, particularly as it was enriched by the wonderful choir led by Stephen Le Prevost (former Assistant Organist at Ely Cathedral and later at Westminster Abbey).

I was in the fortunate position to be able to obtain good financial assistance to assist the Town Church Choir. For about 20 years I was a member of the Oriana Trust, which granted money to causes close to the heart of a Mr. Charles Aeschimann, a wine merchant who had died leaving his money in trust. We met quarterly and continued to support in a small way his favoured charities. However, when the number of Trustees dwindled to just two of us, John Rolph and I decided to close the Trust down and to dispose of the capital sum in accordance with the guidelines of the Trust Deed. Following this decision, on the advice of Advocate Russell Clarke, the two of us granted money to the Ladies College, to Elizabeth College for bursaries, and also £50,000 to the Town Church for the establishment of Choral Scholarships for young people, under the direction of the Director of Music, Stephen Le Prevost.

It is a very 'inclusive' Church and has enjoyed the leadership and preaching of Priests of sound learning and wide vision. During the Covid 19 pandemic in 2020 and 2021 the Church had to close for many months and the worship was zoomed to our homes, and Wendy and I were able to share fully in the worship and also the celebration of Holy Communion, using the Communion set that Wendy had given me when I entered the Ministry of the Church on leaving College in 1961.

Three particular blessings sprang unexpectedly from the lockdown caused by the Covid 19 Pandemic. Firstly, in order not to remain confined constantly to our Apartment, as soon as it was permitted for us to take a walk we made certain that we not only queued, keeping our distance, and shopped for ourselves at last, (Julian had been doing our shopping), but we went walking for a couple of miles every day, most frequently along our favourite route at Pleinmont to the 'fairy ring'; and we observed closely the changing scene as the seasons progressed. Secondly, I began spending more time playing with words, which is another way of saying that I started writing poetry more often. I had long enjoyed putting pencil to paper whilst away on holiday, inevitably strictly following rhythm and rhyme, for that is my thing; but now I penned a lot more poems, some of a religious nature, and many limericks. Thirdly, and most precious, every Sunday morning I enjoyed spending zoom time with Carys and our two granddaughters, Freya, aged thirteen at that time, and Robyn who was ten. Freya was doing well at her Comprehensive School, and particularly in German; so, I started her off on learning French. It meant that on entering year 10 she could merge with a group who had already done three years of French. She in the end gained top grades at GCSE in not only German, but also French. As for Robyn, I started her off on German, because she was contemplating moving at age 11 to a State-run International School where it might be valuable. She also enjoyed the experience; and it meant that despite the distance and the pandemic we were able to maintain a close bond with the two youngest of our five wonderful grandchildren.

For forty years I had enjoyed singing with the Guernsey Choral Society and Orchestra under the leadership of several gifted conductors, particularly under the baton of Alan Gough, often travelling with the choir to perform in France. With a deteriorating voice however, in 2021 I joined Wendy who had retired two years earlier.

For two years, to try and retain a smidgeon of fitness I played table-tennis for two hours each Saturday morning at Guernsey's smart Centre. I was surprised that I could still play reasonably well, but soon decided that discretion was the better part of valour and stopped playing due to advancing age at 87 in 2022.

To my surprise I was approached by a good friend and former colleague, Chris Claxton, who is a gifted composer of mainly church music. One task he set himself every other year was to compose an hour's musical meditation for St Andrew's Church for Good Friday. He invited me to compose words for this meditation on two occasions. With a small choir and orchestra our first presentation was deferred, due to the Covid 19 pandemic, until 2022. It was called "All for our salvation" and was well attended and well received. The second, due for 2024 is "Jesus, the True Bread and the Living Water." It's performance has sadly had to be deferred because of the death of Chris from cancer, early in the year. He will be greatly missed. A man of great faith. These two short cantatas required a lot of thought, but I was gripped by the challenge, moved by the inspiration I felt, and humbled by Chris's response to the words I had written.

Another great joy for both Wendy and me in retirement was to witness the achievements of our three children. Julian became a Chartered Accountant and finished as a Director of the Guernsey Finance Company Louvre. Clare became a Director of Kingston University, and Carys, a professional soloist and consort singer with recording groups such as The Sixteen, the Clerks Groups, and the Gabrielli Consort, later has become tutor to individual Choral Scholars at various of the Oxford Colleges and auditioner and tutor with the National Youth Choir

ONLY JUST

10 CREDO

Inspired by the final chapter in a recently published book by Bishop Richard Harries entitled "The Shaping of a Soul", I feel somewhat impelled, as he was, to outline how it is that I have come to believe the things that I believe, and how I would explain or justify holding such beliefs. Like him, as I contemplate and gaze at the mystery of the universe and all that is in it, I sometimes wonder why there is not complete nothingness, why anything at all should exist.

For me this contemplation began at the age of about fourteen on a calm, starlit night shortly after my grandmother had died and my parents had moved house so that we then began living out in the Gloucestershire countryside in the village of Twigworth. Never before had I seen such a peppering of stars so clearly, and it made me begin to think about the vastness of space and the multitude of stars within our galaxy. Already I had learnt at school that ours was but one of countless galaxies and that space was measured in millions of light-years. It was early Autumn, and I was standing between the outdoor privy, the back wall of the house and the small gate to the meadow where slept our nine

Friesian cows. If all the vastness of what I could see as I gazed upwards was only a tiny fraction of all that existed, there had to be something and some reason for it all to exist. Why was there not nothingness? And why was I, a very minute and extremely insignificant mortal, existing, and why was I free and able to begin contemplating this vast, unfathomable mystery. I suppose it possibly had something to do with the onset of puberty and may-be the fact that I had been attending Methodist confirmation classes; but it was for me a landmark and a vivid, memorable experience of awe and wonder.

Years later at Theological College of course I came to understand this to have probably been a personal leaning towards the first of the three major so-called "Proofs for the existence of God" propounded first by St Anselm in the eleventh century (and endorsed by St Thomas Aquinas in the thirteenth century), namely the "Cosmological Argument", all three of which had been debunked long ago by learned philosophers. When discussing the Christian Faith with Sixth Formers at Stafford Girls High School in the 1960's and at Elizabeth College in the 1970's the students seemed to appreciate my attempts at outlining and then destroying each of the three 'Arguments'; whereupon we would inevitably be placed in the position of considering the alternative to proof, namely FAITH.

The Cosmological Argument stated that everything that exists has a cause, and that there must have been a first cause, and that first cause we can call 'God'. It is countered by the realisation that just because one has never known anything to exist that has not had a cause does not mean to say that such a thing does not or could not exist. Similarly, the Teleological and Ontological arguments can be shown logically not to hold water. They are certainly not proofs for the existence of an Almighty power behind this universe. Nonetheless it is not unreasonable, in my judgement, to cling to such insights as helpful evidence pointing to the existence of such an almighty, creative power or being. Put at its simplest, as one contemplates the beauties of nature it seems to me not at all unreasonable to move beyond "Twinkle, twinkle little star, how I wonder what you are" to "All things bright and beautiful, all creatures great and small, all things wise and wonderful, the Lord God made them all;" although that movement involves an application of faith, which I have come to believe is a most precious, precious gift.

Other such moving moments of metaphysical awe and wonder have, for me, been times of ecstasy in human love, (in particular the time of falling deeply in love with Wendy at the age of twenty-three) or experiences witnessing the miracle of the birth of a baby, especially the arrival of our firstborn child, Julian, and being present at the arrival of Clare and Carys. Never have I driven with such anxiety, trepidation and caution as I did when in March 1963, I drove the two miles home in our Morris 1000, in bitter weather, from Stroud Maternity Hospital to our Manse in Stonehouse, with Wendy beside me, and baby Julian in an unsecured carrycot resting on the back seat. Seatbelts had not been invented. We had suddenly been transformed from being a young married couple into a family, with all its responsibilities, by the amazing miracle of birth, the precious gift of a new life. Other such experiences, for me, have been associated with certain performances of classical music or with corporate singing, though for other people they may come through art, drama, theatre, reading, design, composition, creativity, achievement, the beauties of nature, or through countless other means and sources. Particularly when being creative, people sometimes seem to have the experience of timelessness; for me it has been when attempting to compose poetry, and despite the poor quality of most of my words, just occasionally something is produced that I feel has been somewhat and somehow inspired; but "why?" and "by whom?" I ask.

One particular occasion for me was whilst rehearsing Mozart's Requiem with the Guernsey Choral and Orchestral Society. I was well acquainted with the tenor line, having rehearsed and sung it many times. The conductor Stephen Le Prevost caused us to stand in groups of four, so I found myself no longer in the company of half a dozen tenors. The enclave of four-part harmony to which I was contributing was all-embracing and somehow one was elevated or transferred to another plain, a superior realm.

Over the years I have come increasingly to suspect that we humans have a kind of sixth sense which, unlike the other five, is visceral, and way beyond the physical. As a young teenager I thought I first possibly felt it as a timeless or eternal sensation, for example, when a brilliant winning goal was scored in the final few minutes of a game of football. One was taken out of oneself, and the feeling was amplified by the presence of others around who felt exactly the same elation at the same moment. But if I had left the football ground before the goal was scored and simply read the result of the match in the newspaper or heard it on the radio, I would certainly have been delighted, but would never have known that timeless, out of the body sensation of joy and glory.

Since time immemorial all peoples and tribes seem to have sensed something of the 'other', have felt something 'numinous' which has taken them out of themselves and given them a wish to worship something or someone in a realm beyond that in which they lived their daily lives. It led people to worship, for example, the sun, the moon, the lightning, and thunder or to invent gods on whom to hang their experiences or emotions, such as success, failure, love, joy, fear, victory and many others.

However, I have often found it helpful to approach the subject of the 'other' from a totally different direction, namely from that of our human quests and longings for justice, for love, for truth, for goodness, for quality, for beauty, for what is right, and for freedom. Every parent of more than one child will frequently have heard from one or another child the familiar words "It isn't fair," for from a very young age we all have within us a belief that there should be fairness and that things should be equitable and just. As a Headmaster I used to hear that phrase many times on a daily basis. One doesn't have to be taught the concept of fairness and justice; one is born with it as part of our egocentric, self-preserving nature. Some would identify it as being part of our 'fallen' human nature that is encapsulated within the Adam and Eve myth in the Old Testament. Of course, it is often stated that life itself, basically, is not fair, for the good often suffer whilst the wicked seem frequently to prosper. But just as there is an answer to human hunger and thirst, namely in the provision of food and drink, so also, it seems to me that there must be an ultimate answer to our inborn quest for justice; surely there must be such a thing as 'ultimate', 'absolute' or 'divine' justice.

Similarly, we all feel the need to try and work out what is good or what is right or best or preferable in any situation. We may each come to very different conclusions as to what in fact is right and what is good, both in what we ourselves and in what other people are doing. But the very fact that we have within us that inborn quest, I have come to believe, is more than simply one of the functional abilities of our brains. There seems to me to be some ultimate, absolute right and good towards which we were created to aspire. Likewise, I feel there must be some ultimate truth which enables us always to want to dig and delve until we find it, for we have a yearning, a longing, when faced with any conundrum, crime, puzzle or mystery, to discover what is the truth. Likewise, we each have a unique sense as to what we regard as beautiful, as well as a preference for it, preferring beauty to ugliness, and harmony to discord, knowledge to ignorance, and wisdom to folly. We have differing opinions and views on these matters; but the fact that we have a quest or a yearning or even just a discernment or preference in these matters suggests to me that there must be an ultimate, an 'absolute' (or a divine) beauty, knowledge and wisdom towards which we feel the need to aspire. Then we come to the experience of 'love' in all its varieties, without which the human race could not continue or exist. It is certainly not a concrete thing. It cannot be measured or scientifically proved, but it can certainly be received, given, experienced and known. It is in fact something very real and deeply spiritual, and it points us to something beyond this life and, as I see it, it stems from the source of our very being and points us towards the eternal. We are social beings with a need and ability to relate to others. Freedom is another thing of which everyone senses a need; yet life in many ways constantly seems to restrict our freedom; shortage of opportunity, lack of means and resources, legal restraints and personal responsibilities all combine to put limits on our freedom. Could it not be that there is an ultimate or absolute freedom beyond all things, towards which we can aspire?

These are some of the issues which religions of all kinds down the centuries and millennia have sought to address. It is the six-thousand-year-old Hebrew religion, the precursor and foundation of Judaism, Christianity and Islam, that captured the imagination and won the hearts and minds of millions, for with ancient myths as well as through recorded historical events it tells of a people's search for the divine, which they invariably discovered and came to believe, was the divine's chosen revelation of Himself to humankind. They so believed in a God who was a God of Justice that they sought to discern what that justice might tell them, and then through Moses discovered that God revealed essential commandments and laws for their peaceful, civilised human existence. They sensed that behind the wonders of creation there must be a divine Creator, and through the trials and tribulations of exile and captivity they acquired myths which contain hidden truths about creation and about human nature, and they sensed that God himself had revealed these truths to them for a purpose. Furthermore, at times they even concluded that it was by divine intention that they may have even suffered defeat and captivity, in order that they might begin to discern the nature of true freedom. They then at last began to sense that the very source of all love was embracing and covenanting with their people for a world-wide purpose, and for the benefit of the whole of humankind.

As I reached a stage in my life when I felt the urge and need to pose religious questions, I was fortunate, as we all are, in that one does not start from scratch. Others have felt the same need, and we benefit from their insights, experiences, and writings, as well as from the civilisation and culture into which we are born. Indeed, I knew it would be folly to ignore what had clearly already been revealed to our forebears. I had the great advantage of growing up in a Christian home and in a Church community in which faith was regarded as of very great importance (even though it was conveyed to me in a very narrow, fundamentalist and censorial manner, from which I silently rebelled). It was a faith that had sprung from the ancient Patriarchs and been channeled and developed in the writings of lawgivers, poets, prophets and evangelists. It was a faith that was seen and believed by Apostles and Gospel writers to be fulfilled in the person of Jesus, the Christ, and even translated into English by a local Gloucestershire martyr, William Tyndale (whose censored translations from the Hebrew and Greek formed the unacknowledged basis of the Authorised Version of the Bible). Clearly, religion and faith can be caught as well as taught. Caught, in my case, despite the strictly literalist, uncritical approach of my parents to the Bible, from which, inwardly and increasingly, I quietly rebelled. I regard myself as extremely fortunate in that I was influenced and encouraged also by other followers of 'The Way' who were open-minded and evolutionist in their theological understanding. They believed that science reveals and will continue to reveal how the universe came into existence, but that it is faith that can explain who and what power was behind it all and continues to sustain it.

At last there appeared the Man from Nazareth, whose very nature and teaching seemed to epitomise, embody and proclaim these very qualities of justice, truth, wisdom, goodness, beauty, and love, and whose life and death became seen as the means by which the human race is brought to true freedom, to fullness of life. Probably the best non-Biblical source to give clear evidence of His life is in the writings of the first century Jewish historian, Josephus, who recorded, "Now there was about this time, Jesus, a wise man, if it be lawful to call him a man, for he was a doer of wonderful works – a teacher of such men as receive the truth with pleasure. He drew over to himself both many of the Jews and many of the gentiles." In fact, I have come to appreciate that there is far more textual evidence for the life of Jesus than there is for any other historical figure from the same era in history. And this is the man who has captured the imagination of millions down the centuries, and whose life and teachings have filtered through peoples' hearts and minds, including many of the greatest philosophers and scientists.

Turning to the three Synoptic Gospels of the New Testament, even taking account of the fact that these did not begin to appear in written form until around thirty years after the events to which they refer, and knowing how details can change over time when stories are recounted and passed on orally, I have found it remarkable that three accounts survived which convey the same picture, the picture of a man who spoke of another realm in terms of God's 'Kingdom', and made the Almighty, transcendent Being very imminent, in fact close enough for him to teach us to call God our 'Father'. He was seen to be fulfilling ancient prophecies and offered a blueprint for a better world order of justice, peace and love. Furthermore, I came to realise that Jesus offered and still offers the means for that new order to be achieved, namely by a change within the hearts of us human beings, a change made possible because of the fact that, despite being hounded to death for blasphemy, His offer of forgiveness from the cross is a divine offering and His spirit is still very much alive. Without that fact, the Church, which grew from his twelve followers' teaching, the Church with all its appalling faults and failures down the centuries, would surely never have survived. Yet survive it has.

Jesus also spoke of another existence or realm beyond this terrestrial one, and in doing so found it necessary to paint pictures in words to enable his listeners to begin to grasp its reality and its nature. It is also essential for all believers to speak using images, symbols and metaphors whenever referring to that eternal sphere that Jesus called 'heaven' or 'paradise'.

At Easter in 1953 when I was still only seventeen I found myself hitchhiking for three weeks from Dusseldorf to Lake Constance and back together with my German pen-friend Wolfgang Ottka , with whom unfortunately I found I had very little in common. Our German teacher, Mr Easterbrook, had received a letter from Wolfgang who was looking for a penfriend. Wolfgang's intention was for us to visit as many ancient sites as possible wherever we went. In our travels we also saw in many places the remaining ruins of bombed out buildings from the war. On Good Friday morning, looking very bedraggled after having slept in a barn, we arrived in the beautiful, medieval, walled town of Rothenburg-ob-der-Tauber, and I felt it appropriate to enter the old Church just as a Service of worship was about to start. To my surprise I was taken to be, at worst, a scruffy vagrant or, at best, an undesirable site-seeing tourist. It was similar to what had happened to me a few days earlier in Cologne Cathedral; I was swiftly escorted out of the Church despite my protestations. I made my way to the wall that circumscribed the small town and climbed up inside its narrow passageway. Looking out 200 yards beyond the wall my eyes fixed on a small hillock on which stood three quite well-established trees. As I stood there for a long time and contemplated, reflecting on what had just happened things began to resonate; to me they were no longer three trees; they became, undeniably, three crosses, and I found myself repeatedly humming to myself, "There is a green hill far away....". I trace back to that moment my belief that in some way my future life and work was to be in the service of the Christian Church. I knew that the Almighty does seek to communicate with us.

Four years at Sheffield University confirmed that belief, for in addition to studying Biblical History and Literature under the world famous Professor F. F. Bruce (as well as German, French and Education) and in addition to joining the time-consuming men's hockey club, I linked up with the very thriving and popular Methodist Society, and in my third year, after spending one Semester at University in Münster/Westphalia, I was elected as its President. Mid-week meetings with high-flying speakers such as Lord Soper, Professor C. A Coulson, Lord Tonypandy (George Thomas, Speaker of the House of Commons), the German Pastor Martin Niemoeller (a survivor of the Nazi concentration camp at Dachau) etc. often attracted up to a hundred members. Hearty, inspirational Sunday worship at Sheffield Victoria Hall was always followed by a bus ride to our Chaplain, Rev Brian O'Gorman's manse, where we sang hymns, discussed, socialised a great deal   and were generously fed. My extreme good fortune in falling in love in 1954 with Wendy, who shared the same faith and encouraged me and supported me in pursuit of what I felt to be my calling, was something I have always believed was providential. This, followed by Theological training in Bristol, Ordination, over sixty years of preaching and leading worship has refined, clarified and confirmed much of what I believe. Now, just as three trees once became for me three crosses, regular attendance in my retirement at Anglican Eucharist sees bread and wine truly bringing the blessings of Christ's life, death and glorious resurrection and the very presence of the one whom we together worship.

I have come to realise more and more that there is huge enrichment to be gained if we look at life through the lens of faith. Just as one cannot know how the bark of a tree feels if one permanently refuses to take one's hands out of one's pockets, or just as youngsters will never learn to swim unless they get into the water and take their feet off the bottom, so too the whole of life is seen differently when we take a leap of faith and start viewing it through the lens of faith.

It was our Golden Wedding in 2011. We deferred our celebration until the following Spring when we cruised in an old Russian ship down the Dnieper River from Kiev to Istanbul. We were required by the Travel Company to sit at dinner every evening with a couple with whom we had little in common. He was a lecturer in dentistry and she his practice nurse. They were not interested in religion or visiting churches but were avid film buffs. They described several films they had recently seen; in particular one which began, it seemed, with long sequences of what appeared to be unintelligible modern art. After a few minutes an usherette approached their seats and suggested they should use some glasses, and she handed a pair to each of them. At the end of the film they asked her how she knew in the dark that they didn't have the required glasses. "Ah," she replied, "they reflect." "That's exactly it," I said, but they didn't understand to what I was referring.

ONLY JUST

THE LENS

Seeing nature's slow evolving, tracing planets fast revolving,
Focused through the lens faith renders, shows them in their fuller splendours.

Gaining disbelief's suspension brings a spiritual dimension,
Gives confusion clear corrective, clarity and true perspective.

Shedding light on imprecision, faith adjusts believers' vision,
Tells with awe enchanting stories, opens eyes to heaven's glories.

Bread and wine, 'though consecrated, leave receivers still unsated,
'til communicants with lenses welcome Christ who comes and cleanses.

Deeds reflecting love and mercy show iconic'ly, conversely,
Presence of the Lord now risen, viewed when witnessed through faith's prism.

Come, Lord, end our indecision; Grant our souls that inner vision,
Thus to see your glories freely, find you in the poor and needy

P.G.L.

I have learnt to be critical and to demythologise as I read the Bible and sing wonderful hymns, particularly many by Methodism's Charles and John Wesley that are steeped in profound theological insights. Choral singing for over forty years and acquiring, thanks to Wendy and our children educating me in things musical, a taste for certain strands of classical music (particularly Baroque, Polyphonic singing, great choral works and String Quartets) have, I believe, often given me glimpses of God's glory.

ONLY JUST

In the 1970's and '80's there was an antique shop in Guernsey's Trinity Square where, in the window, I once saw a very moving 'Sampler', the beautiful work of a young child in the early part of the 19th century, which I could not afford but often wish that I had bought. The words so skillfully and beautifully embroidered were those of an 11th century hymn of Bernard of Clairvaux, which at Guernsey's Town Church is often sung at Choral Evensong. It sums up succinctly, especially in verse four, where I now find myself standing and very richly blessed:

> *Jesu, the very thought of thee with sweetness fills my breast*
> *But sweeter far thy face to see, and in thy presence rest.*

> *Nor voice can sing, nor heart can frame, nor can the memory find*
> *A sweeter sound than thy blest name, O Saviour of mankind.*

> *O hope of every contrite heart, O joy of all the meek,*
> *To those who fall how kind thou art; how good to those who seek.*

> *But what to those who find? Ah! this nor tongue nor pen can show:*
> *The love of Jesus, what it is, none but his loved ones know.*

> *Jesu, our only joy be thou, as thou our prize wilt be;*
> *Jesu, be thou our glory now, and through Eternity.*

Bernard of Clairvaux

11 SERMONS ON SPECIAL OCCASIONS

(342) Civic Service celebrating the anniversary of Guernsey's Liberation Day, Town Church, 9/5/1992.

(376) Crypt School Founders' Day Service, Gloucester Cathedral, 14/7/2008.

(389) Chief Pleas Service for Guernsey's Royal Court at the start of the Legal Year, Town Church, 1/10/2012.

(398) Ecumenical Service in St Martin's Church, Biberach-an-der-Riss, 25/10/2015.

ONLY JUST

Sermon (342) preached at Guernsey's Town Church, at the invitation of Dean Jeffery Fenwick, on Liberation Day, May 9th, 1992.

Isaiah 51:8 "My deliverance will be for ever."

It was a very different kind of day 47 years ago. And how the bells of this church rang out as tears mingled with laughter. The final surrender of the German garrison had been signed aboard H.M.S, Bulldog. Half an hour later the 22 men of the Royal Artillery were greeted with tremendous emotion as they came ashore to take over control of this Island from its 10,000 or more German occupiers.

Those who remember that rejoicing will have known how the Falkland Islanders and the people of Kuwait felt when they were liberated. They will also have understood the emotions of people freed from decades of Communist domination, and the relief and joy on the strained faces of the Beirut hostages John McCarthy, Terry Waite, Tom Sutherland and Jackie Mann when they were freed.

For the Liberation of these Islands was not an isolated, one-off event. It was part of a pattern, - a pattern which spells out a whole philosophy of history.

It can be heard in the words of the prophet Isaiah. He and his people had been dragged hundreds of miles into exile in Babylon. There they were subjugated and demeaned, faced with derision and scorn. The occupation of the Channel Islands lasted 5 years. The exile of Israel lasted 47 years. Rather like Hitler and Stalin in the 20th century, Nebuchrezzar of Babylon felt himself completely exempt from the restraints of morality and compassion, provided he was successful. 47 years later another political dictator emerged on the political scene, overrunning nation after nation. All Jewish exiles were apprehensive, many trembled, some were terrified; but the prophet Isaiah in exile in Babylon foresaw that God would use this ambitious, arrogant nation-builder by the name of Cyrus to return all exiles to their homelands.

You could say it was just politically expedient for Cyrus of Persia to return all exiles to their homes; he required a strong buffer state between himself and his greatest rival, Egypt. But Isaiah said that Cyrus would be the unwitting tool in God's hand to restore freedom to his people and to return them to their homeland. "My deliverance will be forever," he said.

Five centuries later came another great empire, strong in administration, whose rule was supreme. Nothing was to stand in the way of the Roman Emperor. He even declared himself to be a god and disposed of anyone who refused to accept it. And he wanted good means of communication, so he built roads, not like ours that were, it seems, designed by drunken Guernsey-men staggering home on a Saturday night, but straight ones, along which trade could flow, armies could march, and his rule could prevail. Yet along those same roads went persecuted Christians, until eventually the Emperor himself embraced the faith, and the Empire itself crumbled.

In our own time we have seen not only the might of the Nazi war machine brought low, but more recently have witnessed the demise of the Communist Eastern Block and of the Soviet Union itself. In Marxism we had a philosophy more subtle than any before it, claiming that the whole of history was inevitably marching towards the classless society. Yet within the Soviet Union and other countries behind the Iron Curtain there were millions who for 70 years sustained their belief in freedom, and millions who retained their faith in God against one of the harshest of atheist regimes.

You **can** explain it by saying: "Every evil empire has within it the seeds of its own destruction," which it has; or "Here yet again we see a triumph of the human spirit," which we can." Isaiah said," God is using Cyrus, and God's deliverance will be forever." Or, as Winston Churchill said, "People in bondage need never despair; there comes a spark from God knows where."

From the Christian point of view, there is an understanding as to where that spark comes from: - God can bend the fortunes of nations and overthrow the powers of evil; and God uses people of faith and courage to achieve it. For the ultimate outcome of history is not in doubt. The decisive battle has already been fought and won. It was when the powers of darkness mustered their array from all ages and all parts of the globe outside Jerusalem 2,000 years ago. They had the chance to give evil the upper hand for ever, to murder God. All their legions converged on Calvary. How they must have rejoiced at 3 o'clock in the afternoon when they heard the words, "It is finished"; but the victory was not theirs. By "It is finished" he meant "Man's deliverance is complete." For Christians the victory is encapsulated in the events of Easter; for the powers of evil have done their worst, yet the victory was with love, not hate; with good, not evil; with light, not darkness. A broken world is thus being renewed. The war has been won, but there are still dreadful skirmishes and battles to be fought. Ours is the privilege of tracing his victories, acclaiming them (as we are today) and even being used to help achieve them, whether it is rejoicing at our liberation or witnessing the defeat of some other evil power.

ONLY JUST

Since last Liberation Day this Island has lost a great Guernseyman in the person of Raymond Falla, who was certainly used in a remarkable way, - bringing sustenance and life to the Islanders who remained here during the Occupation. He described his own life up until 1940 as that of a "hard-bitten and successful businessman, a materialistic type." But adversity changed all that, so that he became one who with distinction served this community. Travelling thousands of miles in occupied France to obtain food, being in charge of both agriculture and horticulture, living by his wits and with great ingenuity, he helped keep the population alive by obtaining food and seed.

His was a life used by God to achieve his victories over evil. The outcome ultimately of God's reign over human affairs is not in doubt; but there are still vast pockets of resistance to his reign, wherever we see man's inhumanity to man, or where morality and compassion take second place to greed and success; but ours is the privilege of identifying his victories, of acclaiming them and of being allowed to share in them by self-denial or self-sacrifice (as was the case of so many who gave their lives, being used by God to affirm his victory.

God wants to use us, and he can when we rejoice wherever good triumphs over evil, wherever we identify with the sufferings of others, as we deny ourselves for the good of others. We should be able to feel at one with Falkland Islanders, with Kuwaitis, with the people of Afghanistan, with all who strive against evil and oppression, with the former Soviet Republics now freed after 70 years under Soviet control, with the hungry, the dispossessed and cruelly treated wherever in the world they are to be found. Perhaps this is why Guernsey people are generous towards the unfortunate, the downtrodden and the oppressed. They share the plight that once was ours. We proclaim the victory that must be theirs. May we long for and be identified with their victories as much as we longed for our own, - knowing that it will come (but only perhaps at great personal cost), and that in doing so we are on the victory side.

Sermon (376) preached at the Crypt School Founders' Day in Gloucester Cathedral, 14th July 2008.

Colossians 1:17 "All things are held together in Him".

I count it a great privilege to be standing here, and it is a particular pleasure to hear the choir in such good voice. I spent 11 years at the Crypt, and for all that time I was a member of the Choir. It was led by the late Harry Dawes. I joined what was then the Junior School on the day the building at Podsmead opened, (in September 1943). Since leaving I've served as a School Chaplain and as a Headmaster; and now serve within Her Majesty's judicial system. I firmly believe in the importance of young people striving to achieve their full potential in academic, artistic and sporting areas of school life; but it is my experience that intelligence and academic achievement don't automatically guarantee a happy, worthwhile and fulfilled life that benefits society and the world in which we live. In my present work in the courts of law I occasionally see young people whose education has simply given them skills that have made them into more sophisticated criminals. What is of core importance is the sort of people we become, the system of values we espouse, our philosophy of life, our beliefs; and these lie at the heart of what happens in schools, for it is in school, as well as in our homes and elsewhere, that we get help to formulate our values, for better or worse.

Two years ago, the Tomlinson Report referred to Maths, English and IT as the core curriculum. These subjects are of course basic. They are essential for much other learning. Without them the door is closed to many other subjects. But to call them the 'core' is a mistake. A core is always what holds things together, the central, important framework. It contains seeds for life.

Six months ago, my wife and I accompanied our granddaughter to a most fascinating lecture at the Bafta Headquarters in Piccadilly. It was given by Tristram Oliver, the Director of Filming of the Wallace and Grommet films, - films such as "The curse of the Ware Rabbit" and "Chicken Run". There in front of us were some of the original puppets, most of them apparently just made out of plasticine. But they're not. Costing up to £32,000 each they couldn't be. No. Plasticine by itself would be top heavy, would collapse or fail to balance. Each puppet in fact has a very strong, intricate, metal skeleton or armature, around which the figure is moulded. The armature has ball sockets for every joint in its body, to make it malleable, yet sturdy and strong, and so that it can stand and balance at whatever angle the animator requires for a given shot.

This armature is the core. The core gives strength and stability; it holds things together. It makes balance and direction possible. Every civilisation, every society, every institution needs a strong core, otherwise it collapses. The core of our Western civilisation consists of its values of liberty, democracy, the rule of law and respect for human rights; and civilisations fall into decline when they lose their moral purpose. School communities also need a strong core, and so do our individual lives. There is something even more fundamental than English, Maths and IT. I know Maths offers a way of thinking rigorously, and numeracy is vital in just about everything we do, whether it's playing darts or visiting the supermarket. But in what way can Maths or English be said to be the core to understanding life? I'm a person, but I don't think the most important thing about me is that I am **one** person. Numbers are part of a complex creation, but their ultimate meaning lies beyond Maths. English is similar, but we need something outside of English to decide the value of literature. There is another core, one that puts the subject in a deeper perspective. Including IT as core seems odd! It seems to suggest that most people before 1980 were not educated. So, I find it hard to see these 3 subjects as the thing that holds everything at the epicentre of an education system. The question of what makes everything hang together, what gives shape and meaning, is a much more philosophical, ethical and spiritual one.

The Founders of the Crypt School in 1539, John and Joan Cook, of course wanted to establish a school free from monastic control; but they nonetheless, like other founders and benefactors of British Education started from the core belief that the universe and we human beings, are part of an ordered whole, created in love by Almighty God, who structured everything with meaning and value. That's why Science, English, Maths are possible. One Biblical writer, St. Paul, (Col.1:17) claims breathtakingly that Jesus Christ is himself the one in whom all things hold together. As Religious Commentator Elaine Storkey has pointed out, a real core curriculum should give every student the opportunity firstly to explore this issue; and secondly to experience the concept through the whole ethos of the school. For the values seen in the community life, the general ethos of the school, convey moral messages more powerful than any that can be taught by precept. And the sort of person we become is determined by the messages we have picked up and the things we come to believe. Values such as fair play, justice, truth, respect. Values such as altruism, kindness, forgiveness; striving for worthwhile goals that require long-term commitment and endeavour, rather than offering instant rewards, – these are whole school values; so are generosity, self-denial, humility, courage. These are the core; and they all happen to be exemplified in the life and work of the man from Nazareth; and John and Joan Cook were two of His followers. Jesus had the audacious hope of making our world reflect the radiant values of the Kingdom of God. Many of these values are enshrined already in cross-curricular PSHE guidelines; but how much more secure they are if they spring from a life that derives its strength from the eternal source of all love and truth and justice and mercy.

We all sooner or later look back at our school days and recall at least one teacher to whom we are particularly indebted. In my case it was Mr R. C. Easterbrook. He taught Modern Languages. He had been on the staff for 2 years before the war; then during the war he had a distinguished career as an Army Intelligence Officer. He returned to the staff with a passion for reconciliation with Britain's former enemies. He pointed me in the direction of doing something that would be seriously frowned upon today; perhaps because my parents couldn't afford to send me on his school trips abroad to Germany, he encouraged me at the age of 16 or 17 to go off on my own to Düsseldorf to spend 3 weeks hitchhiking with a complete stranger. It opened my eyes not only to the value and fun of speaking German, but more importantly planted seeds of reconciliation, understanding and forgiveness. Tragically, a year later Mr Easterbrook was killed in an air crash at Belfast airport soon after moving from the Crypt to take up a post at the University there. His inspired teaching sprang from his core belief that all nations should live in peace and harmony, and that learning foreign languages could promote understanding and reconciliation.

At one time these values that I refer to were provided by religion. Of course, we all have some capacity for moral discernment whether we are religious or not. But I believe that most people who have a strong set of moral values that they hold independently of any religious faith were brought up and taught by people who had such a faith, or at least their parents were shaped by parents who had it. I think we are running on an unconscious momentum that is informed by religious values, and that we need to recover a religious foundation for the moral values of our society, and that we need to do it within your generation. (The poet Seamus Heaney has said: "Some kind of metaphysic has disappeared from the common life. We are running on an unconscious that is informed by religious values. But I think my youngsters' youngsters won't have that."

John and Joan Cook, both of them in their wills not only made generous provision for the founding and continuance of the Crypt School; they also requested to be buried in the Church of St. Mary de Crypt opposite the statue of John the Baptist. Joan also made provision that annually, on the feast day of St. John the Baptist a red rose should be presented to the Rector of St. Mary de Crypt. I find it very significant that John the Baptist should be their chosen hero or role model; for he was the self-effacing prophet who spent his life courageously, wanting the spotlight to shine not on him but on the one he came to announce. (That is why Christmas Day is fixed at midwinter, when the daylight at last begins to shine for longer; and John the Baptist's Day is at midsummer when the light begins to reduce.) He was essentially self-effacing. His role was to point to the light of the world, Jesus Christ, so that His light might shine more clearly in our world; for, as St. Paul says, "In Him all things hold together."

ONLY JUST

Sermon (389) preached in Guernsey's Town Church at the Annual Chief Pleas Service held at the start of the Judicial Year, 1st October 2012.

"Judge not…"

The French expressionist painter, Georges Rouault, liked to look behind what he called "The spangled garments we all wear". (At Chief Pleas he would have had a field day.) One of the themes of Georges Rouault was CLOWNS. He looked behind the spangled garments, the disguises we put on, and he saw the suffering soul within. At one stage he spent day after day in court painting judges and juries. But instead of simply treating them as symbols of authority or of oppression, he had pity on them. As he put it, *"Toutes les richesses du monde ne pourraient pas me persuader de prendre* la *position de juge";* ("All the riches of the world could not persuade me to take on the position of judge.")

Occasionally, when sitting on the Jurats' Bench one really could identify with that. For sometimes, during a major criminal trial, one became aware of the awesome responsibility of trying to make a judgement about another human being, - a judgement that would affect not only that individual, but also his or her family, as well as any victims of their alleged crime, and their families. It is extremely difficult for Judges and Jurats when so much is at stake, especially when faced with conflicting stories and dubious evidence, presented may-be by eloquent and persuasive Advocates.

I sometimes reflect on the words of Jesus, "Judge not, and you will not be judged; for as you judge others, so will you yourselves be judged." In the light of that saying a few people, Leo Tolstoy among them, have taken the view that we should do away with the whole criminal justice system, -

judges, prisons, the lot. I'm sure that is a very mistaken interpretation of those words. For Almighty God, first and foremost, according to the Abrahamic Religions, is a God of justice; and judging by the thousands of children and young people I encountered in my teaching career, God seemed to have implanted in the heart of every one of them a very powerful, instinctive hunger for justice and fair play. To me, that indicates the existence of a divine imperative, an ultimate justice. *Despite what Richard Dawkins suggests, we are not simply part of nature. Our ideals, hopes, values, dreams, do not arise simply from electrochemical brain processes. To quote the Chief Rabbi, Jonathan Sachs, "There is within us the breath of God. We have immortal longings." One such immortal longing is our hunger to see justice prevail.* (In fact, I occasionally perplexed students and pupils by suggesting to those who were aggrieved or felt things were unfair that they were clearly very close to the heart of the Almighty.) Nor can we agree with Tolstoy on this. The Pentateuch recounts the Children of Israel's constant need of judges. It lists the qualities required of them, gives accounts of those appointed and details some of their judgements; and they were not soft on crime. And our Lord himself made clear his judgement on the actions and behaviour of those Pharisees who distorted truth for personal gain, victimized people, poisoned society in the process, and assumed their judgements reached to eternity.

What our Lord surely meant was that we should never try to make a final moral judgement about another. For a start, we never know fully what goes on in people's hearts and minds. We never know fully what pressures they were under or what real freedom of choice they had.

One person who brought this home to us most clearly in recent years was the investigative journalist Gitta Sereny, who died in June. She had first- hand experience of living under the horrors of Nazism. In her search to understand what leads human beings so readily to embrace violence and immorality she interviewed at great length people such as Hitler's favourite architect, Albrecht Speer. She interviewed criminals such as the Treblinka Lagerkommandant Franz Spangl. She interviewed murderers such as Mary Bell (who at the age of 11 had killed 2 small boys on Tyneside in the 1960s). Gitta Sereny sought to challenge the easy and ignorant division of humans into either good or evil. She was fascinated with the way childhood experience could shape later life. She wanted her readers to put themselves in the position of those who had committed monstrous crimes. She asked, "How would we have behaved (given their background, given their upbringing, given the abuse they had suffered, given the pressures they were under)?" Her probing was frightening sometimes, often disturbing, for she had the ability to show us ourselves.

But furthermore, Gitta Sereny shows us how human beings can change unexpectedly. I was reminded of that, on the day when the invitation to preach at this service arrived; for I was watching the former IRA leader Martin McGinnes shaking hands with Her Majesty the Queen. I also recall something the late Jurat Plummer told me years ago. Sitting regularly as Acting Magistrate, he would see certain characters appearing before him week after week, month after month; and then, strangely, he would never see them again. "They had probably found a new girlfriend who preferred them to go straight." Similarly, Gitta Sereny explored the idea that individuals, however terrible their actions, were not innately and irredeemably evil. She concluded that they each had at least "the potential for regeneration."

Indeed, there is a whole range of reasons why we are never in a position to make moral judgements about others. Nevertheless, every day we do have to make judgements of one kind or another; - whether a person is up to a particular job, for example; whether it is right to take action in a given matter; whether someone is guilty of an offense with which they have been charged; and, for the sake of society, what the appropriate sentence should be. We are judging what they have done. It is often a highly fraught, uncertain business, but it has to be done. For, finite, limited creatures, prone to errors 'though we are, that is our birthright, – or better - that is our birth responsibility. Decision-making, making judgements, is the stuff of life; decisions for which, according to our Christian belief, we are ultimately accountable.

But we are never in a position to make a moral judgement about others, as to whether they are ultimately good or evil. Mercifully for us, that decision belongs elsewhere. Mercifully for us, also, the divine justice to which we are all ultimately accountable is far greater than any court of law. Mercifully for us, divine justice is far more imaginative than the prescriptions of the law. Mercifully for us it is far more generous; it is not risk averse.   Our Lord himself was victimized unreasonably and maliciously, and was unjustly judged, but he could still forgive, still redeem. We know that. But we also know that his sentencing and execution were not allowed to have the last word. To the glory of God, Father, Son and Holy Spirit. Amen.

ONLY JUST

Sermon (398) preached in St Martin's Church, Biberach at an ecumenical service, 25/10/2015.

GERMAN VERSION

Liebe Freunde,

Es ist für mich heute ein Privileg und eine grosse Freude mit Ihnen an diesem Gottesdienst zu teilnehmen. Ich bringe Ihnen herzlichste Grüsse von unserem Bailiff, Sir Richard Collas, auch von unserem stellvertretenden Dekan, Rev. Mike Keirle, der auch Priester unserer Sankt Martins Kirche ist; auch von unserem katholischen Dekan, Father Michael Hoare. Jeder hat mich gebeten, Ihnen seinen eigenen besonderen Gruss zu bringen. Und ich grüsse Sie auch im Namen der Methodistischen Kirche, zu dem ich gehöre.

Was Guernsey betrifft, began die Einleitung zu einem dauerhaften Band zwischen unseren zwei Gemeinden mit den Kirchen. Im Juni 1997 hat die zweite europäische oekumenische Versammlung in Graz, Oesterreich stattgefunden. Ich wurde als Guernseys Stellvertreter dorthin eingeladen. Das Thema der Versammlung war "Versöhnung – Gabe Gottes und Quelle neues Lebens."

Meine heftige Neigung für Versöhnung began als ich 12 Jahre alt war. In der Nähe von unserem Haus in England befand sich einen grossen Lager für deutsche Kriegsgefangene. In 1947 wurden die Gefangene erlaubt jeden Sonntag Nachmittag und Abend ihren Lager zu verlassen, wenn sie zur Kirche gehen wollten. Plötzlich wurde unsere Kirche in Gloucester voller dieser deutschen Soldaten, die ich immer für Feinde gehalten hatte. Ich erinnere mich daran wie das Singen sehr tief und laut und eindrucksvoll war. Aber ich hatte Angst und fühlte mich bedroht. Unser Pastor überredete die Gemeinde dass wir welche von diesen Gefangenen kennenlernen sollten. Deswegen haben meine Eltern mehrere Deutsche jeden Sonntag nach Hause eingeladen, wo meine Mutter ihnen Tee, Kuchen und schottische Pfannkuchen vor dem Abendgottesdienst gab. Einer hiess Reinhold Luther, der aus Wittenberg stammte. Er hat uns gesagt, er war ein weitlaufiger Vervandter des berühmten Martin Luthers. Am 26 Juli '47 habe ich ihn mit einem sehr alten Apparat photographiert,. Dieser Apparat hatte einst dem Bruder meiner Mutter gehört, der im ersten Weltkrieg getötet worden war. Ich habe hier jene Aufnahme noch, und auch die eigenhandige Unterschrift des Reinholds. Jeden Sonntag in jenem Sommer hat er uns Geschenke gebracht (besonders Pantoffel aus Seil), die er während der Woche in seiner Freizeit gemacht hatte. Obgleich er uns versprochen hat, dass er uns nach seiner Zurückschaffung schreiben würde, haben wir leider nie wieder von ihm gehört.

Aber das hat mich etwas über Versöhnung gelehrt. Versöhnung ist eine sehr besondere Gabe Gottes. Sie ist die Quelle neues Lebens. Im folgenden Jahr, 1948, durfte ich in der Schule wählen, ob ich Geographie weiter studieren wollte, oder ob ich ein neues Fach, Deutsch, probieren möchte. Ich habe Deutsch gewählt, - Quelle neues Lebens für mich !

Vor 44 Jahren haben meine Frau und ich und unsere drei Kinder nach Guernsey umgezogen, wo ich auf dem Elizabeth Colleg Theologie und ein bisschen Deutsch gelehrt habe. Dort fing ich an, die Erlebnisse von einigen der 2000 Guernsey Menschen zu hören, die drei ein halb Jahre während des Krieges in Lager Lindele verbracht haben; und unser Kirchenrat hat mich eingeladen mit einer Gruppe zu verbinden, die das Thema der Grazversammlung in die Tat umsetzen wollten. Diese Gruppe hat in 1997 eine Versöhnungswoche organisiert. Seit jenem Tag sind so viele neue Initiativen begonnen, dank der Versöhnungsgabe Gottes.

Wenn auch wir miteinander versöhnt werden, dann nehmen wir willig den echten Geist Gottes an, der alle Menschen durch das Tod und die herrliche Auferstehung seines Sohns, Jesu Christ, versöhnt hat, dem sei Preis und Herrlichkeit immer und ewig. Amen.

ENGLISH TRANSLATION

Dear Friends,

It is a privilege and a joy to be worshipping with you today. I bring you warmest greetings from our Bailiff, Sir Richard Collas, from the Roman Catholic Dean of Guernsey, Fr Michael Hoare, and from our Acting Anglican Dean, Rev Mike Kierle. Each of them has asked me to bring you their greeting. I greet you also from the Methodist Church, to which I belong.

As far as Guernsey is concerned the initiative for forming a permanent link between our two communities began with the Churches. In 1997 the 2nd European Ecumenical Assembly was held in Graz in Austria. I was sent to represent Guernsey. The theme was "Reconciliation. Gift of God and source of new life".

My passion for reconciliation began when I was 12 years old. Close to my home in England there was a large camp for German prisoners of war. In 1947 the prisoners were allowed to leave the camp every Sunday evening if they wanted to go to Church. Our Methodist Church in Gloucester was suddenly full of strong men whom I had always regarded as enemies. I was somewhat frightened and felt rather threatened. Our Minister urged the congregation to get to know some of them. So, my parents invited a group of prisoners home each Sunday, where my mother gave them tea, cakes and Scotch pancakes before the evening service. One was called Reinhold Luther who came from Wittenberg. He told us he was a very distant relative of the famous Martin Luther. I took a photograph of him with my very old box camera, which had once belonged to my mother's brother, who had been killed in the First World War. I still have that photograph here and also Reinhold's autograph. Each Sunday, he brought us gifts, e.g. slippers made of rope, that he had made during the week. Unfortunately, although he promised to write to us, we never heard from him again.

But that taught me a lesson about reconciliation. It is God's gift, and it is a source of new life. The following year, in 1948, at school I had to choose whether I wanted to continue studying Geography or whether I wanted to learn German. I chose German, - source of new life!

44 years ago, we moved to Guernsey, where, at Elizabeth College I taught Divinity and German. There I began to hear about the experiences of some of the 2000 Guernsey people who had spent four and half years during the war in Biberach, and our Council of Churches invited me to join a group who were planning to follow the theme of the Graz Assembly by organising a Week of Reconciliation. Since that day, so many new initiatives have sprung to life, thanks to God's gift of reconciliation.

Whenever we become reconciled with one another we are

embracing as our own the very Spirit of God, who has reconciled all humankind to himself through the death and glorious resurrection of his Son, Jesus Christ, to whom be all praise and glory for ever. Amen.

… ONLY JUST

12 POETRY

ONLY JUST

ADVENT

Dead though the winter and frozen the snow,
Could songbirds know what we don't know?
Scorched though the desert and searing the sand,
Can fragile creatures understand?

> ***Hope is the gift of God's mercy unbound***
> ***And Advent the season in which it is found.***
> ***'No absent God,' our praises tell.***
> ***He comes to us, Emmanuel!***

Dark though the world in its sorrow and grief,
Each Advent candle spells relief.
Visions obscured in the depth of the night,
The watchman waits to hail the light.

"People in darkness need never despair;**
There comes a spark from God knows where."
God indeed knows both the source and the aim:
He fans the embers, tends the flame.

Harsh though the tyrant, his mischief and lies
Hold germs that spawn his own demise.
Scorned though the prophets, derided their throng,
Rejoice! God comes!' is all our song.

** The quotation in verse three is attributed to Sir Winston Churchill

ONLY JUST

THE ASSUMPTION OF
THE BLESSED VIRGIN MARY, August 15th,1985

As we travelled in Crete by bus from Kalives village into Hania on Assumption Day we came upon an horrendous scene.

The crowded bus was in a festive mood,
For heaven knows Bank Holidays are rare.
The manic traffic donned demonic powers
For Hania's Orthodox Assumption Fair.

"Don't look", I shouted. Then the traffic slowed
They knew from my expression what I meant; -
The Cretan widows suddenly fell dumb,
Whose sorrows are considered heaven-sent.

Quite motionless the bleeding body lay.
The motor-bike was shattered, upside-down.
They threw his body on an open truck,
Like carcass meat, transporting him to town.

Yet still the hair-brain drivers diced with death
Assuming regulations weren't for them;
While other travelers felt sublimely safe,
Protected by Assumption's Queen of Heaven.

Somewhere two lives lie ruined in the grief
That may the things most credible destroy.
How could they see conceivably in this,
Not Mary, but God calling to their boy?

ONLY JUST

ATHENS INTERNATIONAL AIRPORT EAST

Flying back from Mykonos we were obliged to spend the night trying to sleep on the floor at the airport.

Entangled on the grimy marble floor
A dozen sleeping children lay, at least,
Attracting hungry flies to lips and face
At Athens International Airport East.

Like baby rats, their limbs were intertwined
So much we puzzled long to ascertain
To which child's body arms and legs belonged,
Each kicking each in one reacting chain.

Such scenes should stay on television news
Or overseas where poverty is rife.
How dare such squalor occupy our space.
Why must the Third World interrupt our life?

ONLY JUST

BREAD

Earth and soil, with sun and rain,
Heat and light, we sow the grain;
Soon with wonder witness seed
Germinate for human need.

Flour and water, salt and yeast,
Staple, wholesome, basic feast;
Pummel, knead and leave to rise,
Mould and bake what God supplies.

He provides within his care
Bread for all the world to share.
Should some thirst, in hunger dwell, *(Romans 12:20)*
Feed the enemy as well.

Borrowed from our children's birth,
We did not inherit earth.
God created. Stewards, we
Hold responsibility

ONLY JUST

BY GRACE

By grace there is bread for the breaking,
You gave it and we shall receive.
This food you prepared to bring wholeness to all
Transmutes for us who believe:
Unseen and spiritual riches
No mind upon earth can e'er hope to conceive:
Your ovine sacrificed body
Our guilt and our shame by your grace will relieve.

Through faith may bread with your presence
At each of our Eucharist meals
Bring truth to bear on our values,
Give body to all our ideals,
Knead substance into our dreaming,
Make visions arise into life and be real.
May we your well-giving waters
Your saving presence and fellowship feel.

ONLY JUST

CHURCHGOING

"You've witnessed his removal from the safe, -
Your puny god!
His time for dusting down well overdue.
Such bouncing him upon your knees ensures
He's still a white, Male, Anglo-Saxon Christian like you."
"You've plied your social hobby, - singing hymns
With fervent voice
Of missionary outreach to the poor
Believing your wellbeing now ensures
Beyond all doubt
The future of his people is secure."
"You've visited your own like-minded friends'
Exclusive club,
And shared their self-indulgent little game,-
Dry sandwiches of word and tune ensure,
All unrehearsed,
New generations will consume the same."
We've heard such mouthings. But, whilst God disdains
Security,
These jibes discount his resurrected lives,
Whose hybrids, sprouting from the dung, ensure,
Like Luther Kings
And saints that bear a cross, His Kingdom thrives.

CREATOR OF THE UNIVERSE

Will countless atoms rightly gel
By chance to form a living cell,
And modify through plant and shoal,
And then emerge a living soul ?
God crafts the mutant human frame,
That we may apprehend his name,
Transforming fleeting, earthly days
With glory glimpses of his ways.

Creator of the universe, our Maker and our King,
You point us to the mystery in every living thing.
Your Son is our Redeemer, and our vision is restored.
We share his new creation, and we worship him as Lord.

No process of the brain explains
Our values, hopes, ideals and aims.
Such fragrance stems from soul and heart,
For more than nature are we part.
This truth God each believer gives:-
'The breath of God within us lives.'
Beyond our physical attire,
Our spirits may to heaven aspire.

ONLY JUST

DEEP WITHIN

(Matthew 5:6 "Blessed are those who hunger and thirst to see right prevail; they shall be satisfied.")

(John 6:35 "Whoever comes to me will never be hungry, and whoever believes in me will never thirst.")

Deep within, for fairness there's a hunger,
Rooted that we all may freely dine.
Sing, for an epiphany is witnessed, -
Justice in the countenance divine.
Recognising acts of human kindness,
Knowing how of love we are in need,
Sing with all who source the hidden answer, -
God's eternal love on which to feed.

Deep within the heart, a thirst for knowledge,
Planted that the world may come and drink.
Sing, for it is matched by God's creation;
Wisdom gives a providential link.
Instinct's search for clues to each conundrum
Plumbs the counterbalance of the Lord:
Absolute the truth within his nature
Ever be the truth of God adored.

Deep within, appreciating beauty
Always finds a better one persists.
Sing with all who see this revelation, -
Ultimate perfection - exists!
Hunger then for signs along the journey.
Thirst with us for clues along the way,-
Antidotes to doubt for all to savour
Sing and feast on righteousness today.

ONLY JUST

Deep within, a hunger yearns for freedom,
Longings to imbibe and quench a thirst.
Jesus to the penitent brought pardon;
Bondage in the sepulchre was burst.
Praise the source and answer to our longings,
Alpha and Omega of our need.
Feast on all his bountiful provision.
Alleluia! Mighty God indeed!

DO THEY?

Do tutors lack knowledge? Do bottom clubs win?
Headteachers make errors? Or clergymen sin?
Do dustmen drop litter? Do waitresses tip?
Agnostics start praying? Psychiatrists flip?
Do sailors get seasick? Do Christies sell fakes?
Do bankers make losses? Accountants mistakes?
Do rich men go bankrupt? Do lovers pretend?
Do dancers make faux-pas? Do judges offend?
Do drunkards drink water? Can butchers stay slim?
Do lawyers break secrets? Or surgeons a limb?
Do misers lend money? Or miners go cold?
Do dentists need fillings? Or babies grow old?
Are astronauts earthbound? Can misfits belong?
Night-watchmen start dozing? Can parents be wrong?
Do nurses need nursing? Can doctors be ill?
Do we cease to love? "Yes. But one never will."

DOCTOR DICK

Old Doctor Dick was well esteemed by all except his wife.
She scorned his popularity and mocked his busy life.
He therefore compromised the truth he feared she may despise;
He hid from her his whereabouts and took to telling lies.

So when the Women's Institute invited him to speak
On 'Sex for Over Sixty-Fives' he pondered for a week,
Then told his wife that 'Sailing' was the topic they'd supplied:
"What! Sailing? – You're ridiculous! – You've hardly ever tried!"

"I've been out twice," he said, "and that will get me off the hook;
And where I lack experience, I'll take it from a book."

One day she met a lady who announced to her with pride
That his address had changed her life! She, scoffingly replied:-
"He's only ever tried it twice! That's typical of Dick!
The first time he went overboard; The second he was sick!"

ONLY JUST

EASTER PAEAN

Sing Alleluia! Comes the day
This year again repeated.
Rejoice we all, for Christ is risen!
Our Lord has death defeated.

Alleluia! Alleluia! Alleluia!.........

The membrane of the veil is torn,
To doubters' consternation,
And split the stone-like shell that hails
In Christ a new creation

Our Lord is risen! He's risen for us!
Turned mourning into feasting.
The pest of death is nutrified.
Come, worship without ceasing!

The alchemies of Spring engage:
The bursting bud sings praises,
The skipping lamb rejoices as
The Church her voices raises.

No more we lonely furrows plough,
His loving presence with us;
Wide open are the gates of heaven,
This Easter joy to give us.

ONLY JUST

EUCHARIST

Our loved one planted choicest vines;
now briars have taken root.
The vines are blighted. This prevents
His vineyard yielding fruit.

He looked for judgement, but behold,
oppression and a lie.
He looked for righteousness, but lo,
an agonising cry.

Our God so loved the world he made,
despite our sin and strife,
He sent his one and only Son
to share with us his life.

The ovine Shepherd of our souls
and Guardian of his flocks
Became our sacrificial Lamb.
Supernal paradox!

Good Shepherd, who at Cana's feast
changed water into wine,
Have now transfigured once for us
as Paschal lamb divine.

You, Jesus, at the Supper board
thus caused the wine and bread
To be your blood and body,
and our souls divinely fed.

ONLY JUST

So come, O fruit of yielding vine,
matured in soil and sand,
Distil in us your life divine
through work of human hand.

This song was set to music by Chris Claxton for his 2022 Good Friday musical meditation entitled 'All for our Salvation', performed by choir and orchestra at St Andrews Church, Guernsey

FLIRTING

Flirting is not for teenagers!
It's wasted on youngsters who are;
If accepted they're so trigger-happy;
When spurned, they just sulk in the bar.

Life's squandered on men from their twenties
To forties and fifties who flirt!
They're boosting an inflated ego,
Or offended and dreadfully hurt.

No! The age for making advances
Is eighty! So be not deceived!
For if she says 'yes' you are flattered,
And if she says 'no,' you're relieved.

FRED'S DREAM COME TRUE

This ninety-three-year-old went to a party
Where he danced with a beautiful blond.
They were compatible right from the outset
And enjoyed a remarkable bond.

She was young and extremely attractive
And her rhythm and steps were just right,
So they danced throughout most of the evening
And continued well into the night.

In the morning Fred went to Confession
And explained to the Priest what he'd done:
How, especially when rocking and jiving,
They had had such incredible fun.

"I've not seen you before at Confession;
So why now?" asked the Priest. Fred said "Oh!
I'm a Methodist, but does it matter?
I just want everybody to know!"

ONLY JUST

Grace for Guernsey's Judges' and Jurats' Celebration Meal on the occasion of the Platinum Jubilee of Her Majesty Queen Elizabeth II's Coronation, June 5th, 2022

On this remarkable Platinum Jubilee
Trusting, O Lord, that our purpose is plain,
Judges and Jurats from this Crown Dependency
Hail Queen Elizabeth's glorious reign.

We, in her service, have sworn our allegiance,
All give you thanks for our Sovereign, the Queen;
All have admired her commitment to duty,
All of us praise the example she's been.

Some have known only the reign of Elizabeth,
Some have lived under reigns one, two or three.
Some of us feel we are well past our sell-by date,
Quite out of touch, who've seen four reigns, like me.

She'll now be eating a marmalade sandwich,
Listening to music, the pipes and the drums;
But, with her staff on a five-day vacation
She'll hope that the corgis will pick up the crumbs.

Now as we gather to mark this occasion,
Trusting our merriment brings no rebuke,
Lord, will you bless both this meal and our Sovereign.
Long may she reign as our Queen and our Duke.

ONLY JUST

Grace for the delayed Guernsey Jurats' Retirement Lunch for Sir Richard Collas and Judge Russell Finch

We thank you, Lord, whose realm is vast
That we can have this meal at last.
So, we give thanks for food and friends.
Your bounty, Father, never ends. Amen.
Now, while you've got our full attention
There's just one thing we'd like to mention:
Two Judges, Lord, whom we've admired
Have very recently retired.
The way they both have earned their crust is
In administering justice.
They've dealt with cases short and long
And taught offenders right from wrong.
You'll know, at times such work is boring;
For it's the kind of work that you're in.
They're both as wise, we Jurats think,
As Solomon and Doctor Brink.

They've worked their socks off, done their best,
Kept up to date and kept abreast
Of modern terms like 'cool' and 'woke'
Without regarding them a joke
And acronyms both old and new
Including L.G.B.T.Q.
So, Lord, we have just one requirement:-
You'll grant them joy and long retirement;
And when they come before your court,
Pray, treat them as we think you ought.
So bless this meal, this food and drink,
And both our guests, - and Doctor Brink.

(Dr Brink was Medical Officer of Health during the Covid 19 Pandemic)

ONLY JUST

GRANNY'S REMEDY

When she asked Dr. Jones for some birth-control pills
    At the Clinic on Saturday last,
He just laughed and embarrassed her, pointing it out
    That her child-bearing years were well past.

Well, she knew that already, so he didn't need
    To poke fun at her age on the cheap,
So she told him how, since her dear husband had died,
    Those pills, - they had helped her to sleep.

He said, "Birth-control pills won't assist you with sleep,"
    But she told him she knew she was right.
"I dissolve them, you see, in my grand-daughter's tea,
    Then I find I sleep better at night."

ONLY JUST

THE GUERNSEY 'HEALING MUSIC TRUST'

This scene was witnessed at the Guernsey Residential Home, where Wendy's mother spent her final months

Well sedated, former housewives,
 artists, members of a band,
Dancer, nurse and bus conductor,
 snoozing in cloud cuckoo land.

Most in faded armchairs slouching,
 two in wheel-chairs near the door,
Only sighs and coughs since lunch-time,
 with an intermittent snore.

Stirring, gazing in the distance,
 three more hours then time for bed,
Limbs congealed, impeding movement,
 most communication dead.

Enter, unannounced, musicians
 playing tunes they all can hear,
Bawdy, music-hall, melodic,
 raucous songs from yester-year.

Strings and woodwind with percussion,
 playing just whatever suits,
 Violins, guitars, maracas ,
 banjo, ukulele, flutes.

First the movement of a finger
 taps the rhythm with a sway,
Followed by some recognition,
 "…….dilly-dally on the way!"

Look! A spark is re-ignited,
 pulsing like a metronome,
Locked arthritic wrists are waving
 "……..'cos I can't find my way home."

ONLY JUST

Listen! Now their throats are clearing.
Memories can swiftly be
Resurrected by the tune of
"……..*dream a little dream with me.*"

As one's faith can reawaken
by the words a friend may say,
So their spirits voice their joy
"……..*we'll meet again some sunny day.*"

Just observe the lively scene that
most folk thought could never be,
Animated singing of
"……..*tomorrow, just you wait and see.*"

Sadly, after such enjoyment,
end it does, as end it must.
"Please repeat this transformation,
Guernsey Healing Music Trust!"

Bert, the spokesman for the rest, says,
gently choking back the tears,
"No, I've not enjoyed a session
quite like that for twenty years."

ONLY JUST

HOPE

To people of the Lord whose hope was gone
Who seemed to be marooned in Babylon,
The prophet gave the word of the Lord that he heard,
He told them what would be when God had set them free:

***"The eyes of even the blind will see
And the deaf will be able to hear like me.
The lame will be leaping like deer in Spring
And the dumb will shout and sing."***

They suffered and they wept, oppressed by men
They very seldom slept, were ill, but then
The prophet gave the word of the Lord that he heard,
He told them what would be when God had set them free:

As deaf and dumb were healed by Christ one day
The people all around were heard to say,
"The prophet gave the word of the Lord that he heard,
He told us what would be when God had set us free:"

To suff'rers evermore who have no blame –
The poorest of the poor – tell them the same:
"The prophet gave the word of the Lord that he heard,
He told you what would be when God had set you free:"

To us who pass them by in poverty,
As we turn a blind eye to what we see,
The prophet gives the word of the Lord that he heard,
He tells us what will be when God has set us free:

ONLY JUST

IMPLICATED 1985

A bored Cretan taxi driver offered to give four holiday-makers a day to remember and told us to jump in our car and follow him.

"When I stop, you stop!" he shouted,
full of mischief, raucously,
Short, rotund and bouncy Cretan:
"Get your car and follow me."
Through Kasteli's arid mountains,
heading west towards the sea,
Hair-pin bends negotiating
precipices endlessly.

"Stop the car!" And out he squeezes,
over ditch and bank he leaps,
Fills his arms with sugar melons,
guiltless, down again he creeps.
On he drives, then breaks abruptly; -
Nought his beady eyes escapes;
Never mind who owns the vineyards;
fills his bag with luscious grapes.

Am I aiding and abetting?
Should I be the bounder's guest?
Should we simply follow suit
or make a citizen's arrest?
'Stops to pull wild flowers of ouzo,
aniseed, not by the roots,
Just the yellow flowers to smell.
His preference is stolen fruits.

ONLY JUST

By the caves Agia Sofia
'drinks his colleague's beer galore;
As he coughs and turns his head
he grabs the chance to pinch some more.
Breathlessly he looks for plunder.
Oranges are still too green,
So are pomegranates, lemons; -
olive groves are not his scene.

Passing all the booty to his
passengers now stricken dumb,
Stops the car to gather figs, then
"Fallisana, here we come !"
Straight to the Taverna kitchen!
Jokes his way to take a look
Steals some whitebait, then a plateful,
promising to pay the cook.

What to do with all the loot?
There seems enough to set up stall!
Rascal after lunch for 'afters'
shares them out to one and all.
' Far more fun than driving tourists
tiresomely around the block,
Liberated taxi-driver, free at last to run amok.

All alas are implicated!
They on silver-wedding spree;
We, vacation-time enjoying, -
Glenys, Wendy, John and me.

ONLY JUST

ISAAC'S APOSTASY

Israeli boys have often guessed
they'd make their fortunes in the West;
So that's what brought young Isaac here
and made him richer year on year.
His mother thought it would be good
to pay a visit if she could,
To check that Isaac's English wife
maintained their Jewish way of life.

Immediately, she noticed that
his head bore no distinctive hat.
So, delicately, she expressed
regret at how her son was dressed;
Then asked, in tones somewhat unnerved,
if Jewish food laws were observed:
"I've always, back at home, assumed
that kosher food's what you consumed."

"Well, no!" said Isaac. "Kosher meat
is not what normally we eat.
What's more, we quite like pork and ham!
It's far more flavoursome than lamb!"
Dismayed her dreams had so backfired,
she very furtively enquired:
"You go to synagogue, I trust ?"
"Well, no! I've meetings that I must
Attend and simply cannot miss."
His mother sobbed....... appalled that this,
Her son, had so apostasized:
"My boy, are you still circumcised?"

ONLY JUST

JEREMY'S KITTEN

Young Jeremy's cat had had kittens, but lo,
Only one had survived; so he wanted to know
What to do with it, since it looked sickly; and yet
Neither mother nor father would pay for the vet.

"And you're not having two," said his mother, "you're not!
'Cos you never look after the one that you've got!
In a couple of weeks it must go, and that's that!
You must ask all your friends if they fancy a cat."

…But they didn't! So, not to be left in the lurch,
He decided to make some enquiries at Church.
'Though the kitten was sick, he transported the beast
To the Catholic Church, where he asked for the Priest.

"No, I'm sorry," the Father said, "I would have bitten
Off much more than I chewed if I took in a kitten."
"But its mother's a very good pedigree cat,"
Said the boy; but the Priest had his doubts about that.

"And this kitten's a Catholic one, - very rare,"
Said the lad. So the Priest said he'd offer a prayer
For the health of the animal, hoping that that
Would then fob off the lad and have done with the cat.

Now the following week when the kitten looked sicker
He decided to visit the Anglican Vicar.
"It's a very good Protestant," Jeremy said;
But the Vicar declined with a shake of his head.

Then the Vicar recalled conversations he'd had
With the Priest, who had told him about a young lad

ONLY JUST

Who had claimed that his cat was of Catholic breed:-
"So how come it now follows the Protestant creed ?"

Well, suspecting that now they had fathomed he'd lied,
Very nervously stuttering, Jeremy cried:
Oh! It's easy! It's easy! As easy can be!
'Cos last week it was blind, whereas now it can see!"

KOUSTOYERAKO

During the Second World War after the Germans occupied Crete many local men took to the hills and hid in caves. From there these Partisans carried out daring raids on German positions. A well-known film called "Ill met by moonlight" was made showing the most famous, successful attack undertaken, when five Partisans, led by Leigh Fermor, kidnapped the German General Kreipe. The film was adapted from the book 'The Cretan Runner', by George Psychoundakis. Unfortunately, the Germans decided to take revenge on the village from which several of the Partisans were believed to have come. This village, called Koustoyerako, high up in the White Mountains, is still known as the 'Widow Village', because the Germans rounded up any men they could find and shot them. They then rounded up the women and a firing squad was about to continue this murderous act of retaliation, when a Partisan successfully shot the Captain in charge of the firing squad from a distance of 100 meters. One of the five members of the kidnapping party was Manolis Paterakis. When we were in Crete on holiday with John and Glenys Enticott in 1985 or '86, John encouraged us to drive to this remote village. There we happened to meet Epemenides Paterakis,in a cafe, the 83 year-old brother of Manolis. He took us to his simple home, treated us to heavily salted cucumber, almonds and wine, and showed us the pictures all round his simple room of British and Commonwealth soldiers whom he had helped to conceal in the mountain caves. Epemenides also had another brother who had been the marksman who had shot the Captain. Part of this poem that I wrote was read in English at the funeral of Manolis in Crete.

ONLY JUST

KOUSTOYERAKO

Spiralling, twisting the tortuous journey,
far from the highway, the track and the shore,
Up to the '43 mountain location,
seeking the elderly widows of war:-
Say, eighty-three-year-old, are we intruding?
Why should you gladly your victuals share?
Are just New Zealanders, Aussies and Britons
welcome, or all nationalities, there?
"Do they all find it so hard to interpret
your language, the tears and the pictures in line?
Then do you offer them seeds, nuts and raisins,
moistened with salted cucumber and wine?"
"Which of the White Mountain caves was your shelter
during the 35 days they were there,
Killing all males in revenge for resistance,
shooting five girls in the small village square?"
"Was your own wife one of those who was slaughtered?
Why do you grieve that you had but one son,
Now in Australia, married with children?
Were the two Germans both killed with your gun?"
"Which of your brothers helped kidnap the General?
How did he achieve the impertinent feat?
What was his fate, and was it all worth it,
weaving himself to the folklore of Crete?"
"Forty-three years since the worst of the outrage
there, with the bleak, rugged mountains as host;
Why, Koustoyerako, hide your identity,
having such daring defiance to boast?"
"Here round your table why aren't you partaking,
yet like an aged Apostle preside?
Are you recalling the words of your Christos,-
Fast when the Bridegroom is taken aside '?"
Next to the partisan pictures and family
hangs the Last Supper ere Christ was to die.
"Jesus is eating! Tonight you have feasting!
Epemenides Paterakis, why?"

ONLY JUST

LIGHT A CANDLE

There's just a chance, YOU, as you search,
May hear God's call within this Church.
Less likely, though, for He's not prone
To calling you by mobile phone.

So switch it off, drop what you've brought,
And share with Him some secret thought,
Or light a candle, write a prayer
We'll pray it too when you're not there.

(Of course, you might <u>see</u> <u>Him</u> today
If texting as you drive away!)

ONLY JUST

LOSING ONE'S FACULTIES

Three elderly men were reflecting one day
How each found his faculties fading away;
They knew they were frequently misunderstood
And couldn't achieve what they felt they once could.

The first, in his seventies, found it a bind
That, though he was certainly not going blind,
His sight was impaired, and his hearing as well;
So, too, were his senses of tasting and smell.

The eighty-year-old then recalled how he'd sought
To foster his health by involving in sport;
But despite years of jogging and hours in the gym
He scarcely could walk and could no longer swim.

The ninety-year-old said, "Last night, when I tried
To make love to Maggie, she simply replied:
'We made love ten minutes ago, you and me!'
My problem's I'm losing my memory, you see."

ONLY JUST

MAGI FOREGATHER

Magi foregather, we've studied the heavens!
Saddle your camels and come from afar!
See? A celestial miracle shining!
Come, let us travel and follow the star!

Caspar, bring worshipful incense,
Costly and used of old!
Balthazar, burial perfume;
Melchior, kingly gold!

Don your most regal and stately apparel,
Water the camels. We've no time to lose.
Head for the West, the Jerusalem region,
Search for the baby born King of the Jews.

Herod, the king? He is not to be trusted.
His reputation is tarnished and grim.
Only this Infant is worthy of worship.
Emperors, rulers will bow down to Him.

This is the journey that now we inherit.
Light up your candles, your lanterns and flares!
Sing as we offer Epiphany homage.
Our adoration is added to theirs.

MARY'S LULLABY

Jesus, my baby, the fruit of my womb,
No-one in Bethlehem found us a room.
God will protect you, there's no need to fear.
Sleep very soundly, your Mother is here.

Angels attended, spoke to my soul.
Gabriel told me, 'This is your role:'
"Bring down the mighty, strengthen the weak,
Hold high the humble, Raise up the meek.
Lift up the lowly, root out the proud,
Leave the rich empty, poor ones endowed."

Peacefully sleep in your cradle of hay.
Mary will love you by night and by day,
Sing you this lullaby sent from above,
How you will bring us God's mercy and love,

ONLY JUST

MAUNDY THURSDAY

Urgently threshing and pounding the grain
Promised the slaves' liberation.
Pressing and kneading a leavenless dough
Hastened its panification.

Rescued from bondage that now they may be
Chosen and holy, a nation.
Zion today is united to praise
God for his gift of salvation.

Posting on doorways sanguineous signs
Offered them hope of escaping.
Coating the lintels with marks of the lamb
Showed they were those God was saving.

Passover time came around with the year;
Jesus himself took advantage.
He as the bread of life, He as the Lamb,
Freed all creation from bondage.

"This is my body, and this is my blood:"
Ours is the guilt he was bearing.
RE-memb'ring Jesus, the host and the gift,
His is the life we are sharing.

This song was set to music by Chris Claxton for his 2024 Good Friday
musical meditation at St Andrew's Church, Guernsey

ONLY JUST

ODE TO A SKODA

It was just a gratuitous comment
In jest by a friend who meant well:
He claimed I was making a "statement"
By driving a Skoda Estelle.

As if wanting to know someone's secret,
I wrestled with what it might be;
Was I trying to utter some statement
That truly epitomised me?

Was it "Headteachers' incomes are meagre?"
Or, "Their role undervalued too much?"
Do I scorn the position I'm holding?
Hope to focus attention on such?

There's one Headmaster uses Shanks' pony!
Number two at the Office – a bike!
One cadges a lift from her husband!
Surely people can use what they like!

But if I can be perfectly honest,
I don't ditch a true friend if it clanks;
And, besides loving rusty old relics,
I begrudge paying interest to banks!

ONLY JUST

OLD JOE MCLOWE

Old Joe McLowe, the farmer, had had a rotten year;
His crops were unsuccessful; he'd lost a healthy steer;
His overdraft had doubled; he felt a sense of shame;
His wife had been unfaithful, and he had got the blame;
And then, in height of summer his wife took ill, and died!
He'd had enough, but didn't grieve, it cannot be denied.
Joe went straight to the Press Shop, and this is what he said:
"I want to place this notice: - 'Mabel McLowe is Dead'! "
The lady looked quite puzzled, that after such a loss
He'd used no words of tribute, so went and fetched her boss.
He'd heard of Joe from neighbours, who'd known him from a lad.
He knew about Joe's problems and what a year he'd had;
And so, he made this gesture, (admittedly not large):-
"Joe! Double up the wording! There'll be no extra charge.
Add four more words! We'll print it in Monday evening's Press."
This put Joe in a quandary and under some duress.
He pondered, then dictated, (lest his intention fail),
" 'Mabel McLowe is dead.'"…..plus…." 'One bicycle for sale!

PARADISE

On the island of Mykonos the beach called Paradise (not to be confused with Super-Paradise) is indeed a sunbather's paradise.

Ferries leave from Plati Yalos
frequently for Paradise,
Each direction thirty drachmas,
irresistible the price.

Stockholm never sends the ugly;
elderly remain in Bonn,
Since the judgement in this heaven's
based on one criterion:

ONLY JUST

Sun & wind and tanning lotion
help convert the beetroot skin
To the common hue of heaven,
walnut bodies free from sin.

Campers who prolong the foretaste
find reality is blurred.
"Like a concentration camp"
was someone's verdict overheard.

Everywhere is overcrowded,
mass exposure, endless queues,
Loud obligatory music,
stringent rules and broken loos.

Homeward plough the boats at evening,
smileless every weathered face,
Dehydrated bodies begging
for a sip of saving grace.

Are the resurrected flowers
or the skipper's simple shrine
Not by far a truer earnest,
or his food, his bread and wine?

ONLY JUST

PATIENT 'JACK'

One hospital patient, 'Old Jack',
had tubes in his throat, nose and back;
On a drip, through a wire, he was heard to enquire
"Hey, nurse! Are my testicles black?"

His words made her cheeks go all red;
but she couldn't ignore what he'd said.
Embarrassed, she blushed, then turned round and rushed
To tell Sister, who ran to his bed.

Roared Sister, renowned for her knack
of allowing no messing from Jack,
"Some problem is there? If so, tell me where!"
He replied, "Are my testicles black?"

She flung back the bedclothes to see;
then pulled down his pants to the knee.
She found she could tell, for she studied them well,
They were normal, as normal could be.

When Sister said, "No, they're not black,"
he ripped out the drip, tubes and track.
With anguish he gasped, "That's not what I asked!
I asked, 'Are my test results back?'!"

ONLY JUST

PAUSE, YOU PILGRIMS

Pause, you pilgrims. Give me heed!
Of creatures' blood God has no need.
That your worship ne'er can smart,
Just offer purity of heart.
God requires three things, so firstly:
Heaven calls us to do justly;
Secondly, that we love mercy;
Third, that we walk with him humbly.

Pause, you pilgrims. Give me heed!
For temple shekels there's no need.
Should you bring your foreign change,
Our God will not regard it strange.
You should seek no segregation;
Love shows no discrimination.
God says, "Zion's congregation
Shall consist of every nation."

Pause you pilgrims. Hear my voice!
Since religion is your choice.
Lest God's judgement you invoke,
It must no corruption cloak.
'Blessed are the pure in heart' was
What my message from the start was.
''Pure in heart' for God's elect is
That you have but one objective

This song has been set to music by Chris Claxton in his 2022 Good Friday musical meditation entitled 'All for our Salvation

ONLY JUST

A PRAYER

(John, chapter IV – Jesus at Jacob's well in Sychar)

We pray you, Source of Living Water,
O Lord of life with healing powers.
Come, prime the well that springs a fountain,
And quench this craving thirst of ours.

Too much the celebrated waters
We drink, where luring tastes defile,
Consuming mindlessly the fouling
From wells of double-dealing guile.

So grant us, Lord, the gift you promised
The Gentile at the Jacob well.
Come, wash our stains, then re-direct us,
And all truth's compromises quell.

Lord, feed our parched and wilting spirits,
Whose insight all our substance knows.
Revive us with your living water,
That through our lives your glory shows.

We praise you, resurrected Saviour,
Whose risen life we now can know !
Your earthly font sheds drops of glory;
In heaven will surge its fullest flow.

ONLY JUST

REFLECTING THE LIGHT

When I walk by the shore in the morning
As the sun rises over the sea,
The reflection of light on the water
Casts a ray that's directed at me.

When I walk by the shore in the moonlight
Its reflection is shown on the sea,
But the rays that are traced on the water
Are the sun's way of shining on me.

May the light of the world shine upon us
Like the sun on the moon up above;
We'll reflect then His rays on each other
As we angle our lives to his love.

For whatever we do in the day-time
And wherever we slumber at night,
We are never beyond his attention,
For he wants us reflecting his light.

Jesus said, "Let my light shine about you,
So that people will see your good deeds
And give praise to my Father in heaven,"
For the darkness His radiance needs.

ONLY JUST

(This song is based on a Thought for the Day delivered by Rev Lucy Winket (Rector of St James, Piccadilly) on Radio 4 in 2018. It described human blood as our body's transport system, carrying oxygen to our organs and taking away the waste. She called it a wonder and an everyday miracle of our bodily selves, linking us not only to all other humans but to all blood-filled creatures on earth. This song has been set to music by Chris Claxton that seeks to replicate the beating of the human heart. It was included as 'Precious Lifeblood' in his Good Friday musical meditation entitled 'All for our Salvation' at St Andrew's Church, Guernsey in 2022)

RHYTHM OF THE HEART

Precious lifeblood in the womb pulsating as it starts,
Flowing, energised by living beating hearts;
Shared by every sanguine creature on this earthly ball,
Nothing substitutes in nature, joining one to all.

Beat, my heart, to the rhythm of your glory!
Fill my life with the measure of your story!
Lord, restore your true design!
Fuse your nature into mine
With these gifts of bread and wine!

Vivifying and uniting, crossing each divide,
Bridging border, creed and gender, this shall be our guide.
Potent symbol, so dynamic, life-force flowing free,
This, the blood that our creator gifts to you and me.

Of one blood are all created; even Heaven's Son
Shared our creature life, and thus with us became as one.
His life-giving blood of Heaven, shed for human sin,
By transfusion offers life to all his kith and kin.

ONLY JUST

Come, Lord Jesus, Paschal Lamb, your blood was shed for all..
With this fruit of vine renew us, lest we further fall
Rescue, motivate and strengthen, fill this life of mine,
Flowing, surging, energising with your life divine.

ONLY JUST

The Red Cross ship, the SS Vega, set sail from Lisbon to German occupied Guernsey on 20th December 1944 with a cargo of food and medicine. John Mahy Gallienne (known a P'tit Jacques) painted several images to commemorate the arrival of these desperately needed supplies. Using a technique of reverse painting on glass with metallic foil, known as 'tinsel painting', the image was drawn in ink then in-filled with solid and translucent colours, allowing reflected light from the cigarette packet foil stuck to a backing board to give a shimmering effect.

GUERNSEY'S CHRISTMAS -1944

Moonlit and starlit the nights in December,
Vega conspicuous high overhead,
Little Jacques Gallienne, tinsel-work artist,
Prayed, with the whole population, for bread:

Food for the table to last them the winter.
Humbly he offered his Methodist prayers,
Asked that divine intervention from heaven
Might bring relief from this hunger of theirs.

Churchill's assurances sounded but hollow:
"People in darkness need never despair;"
(Nothing had come of his promised protection):
"There comes a sparking from heaven knows where."

ONLY JUST

Christmas was desolate, Islanders hungered,
Cold and abandoned with morsels contrived.
When, on the morning of twenty and seventh,
Sparkled the rumour: "Red Cross has arrived!"

Soon they were shouting it high from the roof-tops,
Never a voice on the Island was dumb:
"See! It's the Vega, the Red Cross ship Vega,
Brightest of stars in the heavens, has come."

Thus Little Jacques, with his tin-foil and brushes,
Painting on glass he'd acquired on the nod
Pictures, especially that heaven-sent vessel,
Practised his art to the glory of God.

Praise for the science that searches the heavens!
Praise to our God, for the stars he has made!
Praise for the blessings that came with the Vega!
Praise to the Lord, for he comes to our aid!

ONLY JUST

In 1942 two thousand non-native Guernsey residents and their families were deported from the Island at short notice by the German occupying forces and sent to internment camps in Southern Germany. Hitler ordered it in retaliation for the internment of German civilians by the British in independent Iran. The main camp to which the Guernsey deportees were transported was in Biberach, where they endured hunger, cold and much deprivation for over two and half years. Since the end of the Second World War various acts of reconciliation have taken place between the people of Guernsey and Biberach, such that a unique and very special relationship of friendship has developed between the two communities. The Biberach Song is often sung, particularly in association with the week-long street festival known as the 'Schützenfest', depicting ancient medieval crafts, which is often attended by a contingent of Guernsey's 'Friends of Biberach'.

Biberach's Schützenfest Song

German words, verses 1-3, composed by the great poet Christoph Christian Sturm, (1740-1786) The 4th verse and the English translation of verses 1-3 by Peter Lane. Music composed by Justin Heinrich Knecht, (1752-1817))

Thy world, Creator, gleems with beauty!
Such joy abounds in all I see!
Now decked in all their festive clothing
are mountain, valley, woodland, tree.
For me all, all are holy places.
Whate'er my eye or footstep traces
Perceive I, O Creator, Thee;
Where'er in meadowlands I venture,
In each divinely crafted creature,
Father of all, 'tis Thee I see.

ONLY JUST

Each whisp'ring leaf calls out in gladness;
'With joy let all extol the Lord!'
Why dream away your days in sadness?
God's world such beauty doth afford.
Illumined by the dews of morning,
The meadow garden, lake, adorning,
Cry: 'How God blesses each the same!'
The stream shouts, rushing from the mountain,
'God is of goodness source and fountain!'
The brook lisps softly: 'Praise His name!'

Joy abounds now all about me!
Rejoice, my soul with thankfulness
At God's great universal beauty!
Why should he me so richly bless?
Sound ev'ryone abroad His praises
whose bounty wondrously amazes,
With mercies springing from His heart!
Now join the choir of all creation:
To Thee be praise and adoration;
Thou, Lord, Eternal Goodness art!

(Verse 4, by Peter Lane, are his attempt to bring a little 21st Century reality into Sturm's romantic poem.)

But see! How we have marred creation,
Destroyed the trees that cleanse the air,
Polluted rivers, streams and oceans,
Wrought damage in the ozone layer!
Lord, help us all to heed the warning,
Of unrelenting global warming!
Why are we to such dangers blind,
Consuming fossil fuel perversely?
May God haste to our aid in mercy
And wake the will of humankind.

ONLY JUST

Biberach's Schützenfest Song. By Christoph Sturm

Rund um mich her ist alles Freude !
Verschönt ist, Schöpfer, Deine Welt.
Es prangt in seinem Feierkleide Gebirg
und Tal und Wald und Feld.
Wie heilig wird mir jede Stätte !
Wohin ich seh, wohin ich trete,
Erblick ich Dich, o Schöpfer, Dich;
Wohin ich seh auf allen Fluren,
In allen Deinen Kreaturen
Erblick ich, aller Vater, Dich.

Das Murmeln in belaubten Bäumen ruft:
'Freudig müsst Ihr Gott erhöhn!'
Die Zeit in Schwermut zu vertraumen,
ist Gottes Welt zu voll,zu schön.
Mir sagt, beglänzt vom Morgentaue,
die Flur, der Garten und die Aue:
'Wie segnet unser Gott so gern!'
Mir sagt das Rauschen seiner Fluten:
'Gott ist der Urquell alles Guten!'
Der Bach sagt lispelnd: 'Lobt den Herrn!'

Weit um mich her ist alles Freude,
O freu auch, meine Seele, dich
In Gottes schönem Weltgebäude!
Wie reichlich segnet er auch mich!
Lass dessen Lob umher erschallen,
der dir so wohl tut, allen, allen
So wohl tut, der so gütig ist!
Stimmt ein in der Geschöpfe Chöre:
Dir, Gott, sei Preis, Dir Dank und Ehre,
der Du der Ewiggute bist!

ONLY JUST

SHEPHERDS, AWAKE !

Wake up, shepherds, stop your dreaming!
Come and contemplate a world made new.
Otherworldly things have happened!
Don't assume that Christmas-time is not for you.

Swiftly, shepherds, pass your watch to
someone else, or find a friend or two!
Come and gaze in rapt amazement!
Don't assume that Christmas-time is not for you.

Listen, shepherds, lambing season
won't be here for weeks and comes on cue.
God's own Lamb is born to rescue.
Don't assume that Christmas-time is not for you.

Come now, shepherds, sheering time can
wait until the warmer days are due.
Veer your course to David's city.
Don't assume that Christmas-time is not for you.

Hasten, shepherds, end your milking.
Just release the sheep to graze and chew.
Planet earth, through Mary's baby,
Can be rescued! Christmas-time is meant for you!

This song has been set to music by Rev. Nathan Falla and also by Chris Claxton.

ONLY JUST

SHOUT AND SING

To people of the Lord, whose hope was gone,
Who felt they were ignored in Babylon,
Isaiah gave the word of the Lord that he heard.
He told them what would be when God had set them free:

"The eyes of even the blind will see
And the deaf will be able to hear like me.
The lame will be leaping like deer in Spring
And the dumb will shout and sing"

As deaf and dumb were healed by Christ one day
Observers in the crowd were heard to say,
"The prophet gave the word of the Lord that he heard;
He told us what would be when God had set us free:

They crucified the Lord on Calvary Hill;
But even on the cross he loved them still.
They heard the precious words from you know
"Forgive them, for they clearly don't know what they do."

On Resurrection Day the Saviour rose,
Appeared to his disciples, as each one knows.
Now Thomas wasn't there when the Master came,
But even he believed when Jesus called his name.

To unbelievers, doubting the Gospel claim,
Deriders and deniers, tell them the same!
"The prophet gives the word of the Lord that he heard,
He tells them what will be when God has set them free":

This song has been set to music by Chris Claxton.

SOCIETY

Carry on, carry on! You're spending well!
You're bringing in the profit!
If you don't understand society
You'll fall a victim of it.

        Have a drag, have a fag! You'll cool your nerves
                And show your disaffection.
            'matters not if your arteries congeal
                Or you die from lung infection!

Have a sniff, have a fix! You'll find escape!
You will, upon my honour!
What the hell if it wrecks your life and then
Your brain ends up a gonner!

        Bottoms up, drink it up! You'll always get
                Instant excitement from it.
           Never mind if you get psoriasis
                Or expire inhaling vomit!

Get 'em off, have it off! If you can't stand
The limits of your tether,
When you're H.I.V. you can lie with me;
We both can go together!

        Turn the knob, turn it up! Shut out the world!
            Hear sounds the punters wish you!
      There's a chance that your ear-drums won't be harmed
           And neighbours won't take issue.

ONLY JUST

Chop it down, pull it up for extra wood!
The new-found land we'll man it.
Just forget what the lack of oxygen
Is doing to the planet.

                    Rev it up, burn it up! With fossil fuels
                      More speed can now be managed.
                  We shall not be around to face it when
                          The ozone later is damaged.

Carry on, carry on! You're spending well.
You're bringing in the profit.
If you don't understand society
You'll fall a victim of it

ONLY JUST

SPEEDING ON THE MAINLAND

Now old Eugene and Florence had never before left the
Island in which they were known;

But they thought 'twould be nice after 60-odd years to
explore the U.K. on their own.

That meant taking a journey by ferry to Poole, and they'd
drive their old Skoda Estelle;

So the garage attendant checked water and oil, and they filled
up with petrol as well.

With an old Highway Code and a very old map they set off
from Poole, heading east.

They thought they might visit the Chessington Zoo and see
something of London at least.

Soon the traffic police grew extremely concerned, for they
monitor how people drive,

Because something was causing a hold-up somewhere to the
south, on the M25.

So they phoned to their mates at the next interchange, and
they spoke to a sergeant, called Sam:-

"Would you go and investigate what's going on; it appears
there's one hell of a jam!"

ONLY JUST

Well, in no time at all Sam established the cause:
'Contravention of authorised code!'

In the outside lane doing just 25 some old fellow was
hogging the road!

It was Eugene, of course. So Sam forced him to stop. Then
he saw in the passenger seat

An old woman was in a severe state of shock, and her face
was as white as a sheet.

After questioning, Eugene admitted his speed. "But you're
lucky you're both still alive,"

Said Sam. "No we're not," replied Eugene, "look there! M,
for Motor-speed! M25!

"But hang on," answered Sam, "take a look at your wife!
She's a shivering wreck, can't you see?"

"Oh, it's not driving slowly," said Eugene, "caused that; we
have just left the M ninety-three!"

ONLY JUST

JUNE 29th, St. PETER'S DAY ROCK

1

Beside a Galilean beach
was born the greatest work to reach
Mankind, when Christ began to teach
the fishermen ashore.
The first were Andrew, John and James,
who joined when Jesus called their names.
Then Peter heard his brother's claims
and went to learn some more.
He witnessed every word and deed,
and Jesus ordered him to feed
His human flock, whatever need
they had within their hearts.
So Churches founded near the sea
to him may dedicated be
Who cast the Churches' first decree –
to preach in foreign parts.

Chorus

He's the Rock whose Day we celebrate!
He's the Rock whose way we emulate!
He's the Rock whose name we venerate!
He's the 9 a.m. to 5 o'clock Rock!
He's the 8 a.m. to 6 o'clock Rock!
He's the 7 a.m. to 7 o'clock Rock!
He's the 6 a.m. to bed o'clock Rock!
He's the 29th of June o'clock Rock!

2

At Caesarea Philippi Christ called
his 12 disciples nigh
And asked them, could they clarify
who people thought he was.
Some said his mode of ministry

ONLY JUST

was old Elijah's markedly
Or John the Baptist's possibly.
He then explained, "Because
I need to know, can you decide
how I can be identified."
Our Patron Saint himself replied,
"You're God's anointed King!"
"Upon this Rock my Church will stand,"
said Jesus, "and to you I hand
The Keys to help you understand."
So this is why we sing:-

3

At Jesus' trial he was afraid
and by the courtyard fire he stayed,
But there the High Priest's serving maid
accused him blatantly:
"I know I'm right when I connect
your accent with his dialect;
As far as I can recollect,
you come from Galilee.
You can't deny that you were seen
accomp'nying the Nazarene!"
But Peter, shouting words obscene,
did categoric'ly.
He thus disowned the Lord of all,
and hearing thrice the cockerel's call
He wept; it caused him to recall
his Master's prophecy.

4

After Ascension-tide he lost
all doubt and fear at Pentecost,
Assured of resurrection, tossed
all caution from his mind,

ONLY JUST

Ignored the Sanhedrin's request,
preferring God's divine behest,
Announcing Jesus was the best
of every human kind.
In Temple courts he boldly said
that God had raised him from the dead;
Then to Samaria was led,
and to Cornelius.
Escaping from a prison cell
he preached to Gentile folk as well,
And gave to Mark accounts to tell,
who's passed them down to us."

(This song was set to music by Martin Cordall for use on St Peter's Day at St Peter Port School, Guernsey)

ONLY JUST

THAT "CIGARETTE"

Guernsey receives its television from the U.K. by means of a massive mast erected in the Parish of Castel. It resembles an enormous cigarette that reaches into the sky. I reflected on how the one reflected the harm of the other.

Because pollution comes disguised,
Rolled up in man's achieving,
And human progress, tipped with gold,
Ignites our unbelieving,

"Society could still regret that all-pervasive "cigarette".

It furs the arteries of life
In homes of every station,
Demanding full attention from
Its place of exaltation

Despite the night-time warning light
So prominently sited,
Too passively we all ingest
Its values, tarred and blighted.

Insidiously it denies
Us all imagination,
And surreptitiously invades,
To choke all conversation.

It stains the moral finger-nails
With nicotine, comprising
Deposits of persuasion, its
Perversions normalizing.

ONLY JUST

I don't deny the drug's supply
Of aid to education
Nor what it contributes by way
Of healthy information

It helps relax and gratifies
The need for stimulation,
But clogs the lungs with indolence
That breeds an idle nation.

In childhood, when I rolled my own
And rummaged in the attic,
No television mast made me
A media fanatic.

ONLY JUST

THE ANT'S HIGHWAY

Identical, the models race
The route each programmed driver knows,
Surmounting foes and obstacles
Along confusing contraflows

        Head on they meet more of their kind
        And take avoiding action late,
        Dicing with death they brake and swerve
        To keep a frantic dodgem date.

The truckers heave and push their prey
Back home while busybodies peer,
And undertakers, next of kin
Combine to keep the highway clear.

        Removal men deliver eggs
        As if possessed, with twig and husk,
        While taxi-drivers each compete
        For passengers from dawn to dusk.

From way above the camera zooms
Upon our human mayhem scene,
Then speed the film as to reveal
Ourselves as ants might well have been.

        Now shoot the traffic on the track,
        Enlarge the ants' highway by far,
        And see the hair-brain monsters rush.
        Behold the creatures that we are.

ONLY JUST

THE ATHEIST'S PRAYER

An atheist walked through the forest in undergrowth over his knees,
When suddenly, all unexpected, appeared a huge bear through the trees.
In terror, the atheist panicked. He ran just as fast as he could.
The bear, feeling frisky and hungry, pursued him, as any bear would.
It caught him and lunged at his body, and threw the man down on the ground.
Then, licking his lips with some relish, rejoiced at the meal it had found.
The atheist, needing assistance, thought may-be he'd offer a prayer;
But, holding his disbelief sacred, he thought there was nobody there.

But now he was desperate, truly. The bear pressed his paws on his chest.
Its teeth showed great anticipation and pulled at the strings on his vest.
Well, should he become a believer? Hope God could make bears disappear?
He thought it would really be pointless and certainly sound insincere.
He suddenly had an idea his terrible fate to avert:-
The bear might become a good Christian! Not he, but the bear, could convert!
He took up a reverend posture, prayed "God! Cause this bear to believe!"
The bear, putting both paws together, said "F'what we're about to receive................."

ONLY JUST

THE CATHOLIC PRIEST AND THE RABBI

A Catholic Priest and a Rabbi
were travelling once on a bus;
They found they were sitting together,
so started to chat and discuss.
Of course they got onto religion.
The Rabbi referred to his wife
And how they kept strict kosher food-laws.
The Priest described celibate life.

The Priest then enquired, "Are you saying
you've never, not once, tasted pork?"
"Well, just between us," said the Rabbi,
"I once tasted bacon in York.
The conference I was attending
had all kinds of food. We could choose.
In error they brought me some bacon
which wasn't intended for Jews."

So then, feeling somewhat emboldened,
the Rabbi enquired, speaking low,
"I really don't know how to put this;
it's none of my business, I know.
Your celibate life's so demanding;
but, truthfully now, can you say,
You've never made love to a woman?
Not once in your life to this day?

ONLY JUST

"Well, yes! There was just one occasion,
which, as I look back, I deplore.
We're speaking in confidence, aren't we? -
I'd rather not say any more!"
A long, stony silence then followed.
The Rabbi at last gave a wink.
He turned to the Priest and he whispered.......
"Much better than pork, don't you think?"

ONLY JUST

THE FIREWALKERS OF KATARAGAMA

This poem was written after somewhat reluctantly being persuaded to stay up all night to witness the annual 'Walking on Fire'. We had travelled to Sri Lanka to visit a self-supporting orphanage outside Colombo run by Pat Patabomi, a former Buddhist monk, for boys orphaned by fighting in the north. Guernsey schools had raised money to provide electricity for the home and its milking sheds. Pat expressed his appreciation by driving us to visit famous sites and some unusual festivals around the Island.

Devotees in tens of thousands,
bearing fruit of every hue,
All have brought their Lotus flowers;
Buddha has received his due.
On his third Sri Lankan visit
Buddha meditated here.
Hindu Skanda's lance is also
said to be residing near.
Score on score are sleeping soundly
wheresoe'er the eye may roam:
Temple precinct, park or pavement;
earth their pillow, sky their home.
Hundreds more are dozing, resting;
thousands still their sleep forego,
Silent through the long night watches,
waiting for the fire to glow.
Now at last, the flames subsided,
walkers wade the cooling stream,
Deep entranced or meditating,
in their eyes the fire's gleam.
In this Menik Ganga river
countless people come and go,
Purifying and oblating
in the holy water's flow.
Here barefooted pilgrims gather,
as their custom still allows,
Seeking self-mortification,

ONLY JUST

thus repaying solemn vows.
Burgher, Sinhalese and Tamil,
all their warfare well-rehearsed,
Now approach the lonesome journey,
each to quench the daring-thirst.

Young and old of equal sexes
linger long and never tire:
Buddhists, Hindus, Moslems brave the
indiscriminating fire.
Drums are beating tribal rhythms,
frenzied rhythms, faster still.
Hearts are beating, pulsing, pounding,
synchronising fire drill.
Some lift high their fetish symbols,
some hold children in their arms,
Some protect their flowing sarongs,
others cling to lucky charms.
Some race madly, helter-skelter,
gain their goal with lengthy stride;
Others nonchalantly skipping,
cloak their anguish, pain or pride.
Seasoned, weather-beaten women
dance their sari-clad routine,
Jigging strictly to the drumbeats
sounding o'er the silent scene.
Some with Nazi-step defiance
strut their arrogant parade.
Some tread gingerly the embers,
pleased their turn has been delayed.
'Though attendants at the ready
wait for victims of the coals,
Witnessed with such approbation
none admits to burning soles.
Still they come with frantic fervour,
leaping, lurching, striding by.
What fanatical obsession!
Brave the embers! Do or die!

THE LANGUAGE OF HEAVEN

'Kalimera', stutter strangers. 'Kalispera', they intone
Phrases gleaned before departure haltingly from linguaphone.
'Efharisto' to the natives. 'Parakalo' they reply.
Poor attempts at using words they scarcely can identify.

'Me', I point, 'Papas Englesi'. (All pronunciation wrong),
Dipping gingerly the toes in oceans where they don't belong.
'Guten Morgen', 'Guten Abend', 'Danke', 'Bitte' - all reveal,
Dumb with insularity the Englishman's Achilles heel.

Since here's no abiding city and our Babel tongues abound,
Where is fluent, universal, full communication found?
If in art, love, truth or music, how do **we** learn, 'nimm doch Acht'
Zion's Esperanto ere the 'Kalinichta', 'Gute Nacht'?

ONLY JUST

It was our Golden Wedding on July 29th, 2011. In celebration, the following Spring we journeyed along the Dnieper River on a cruise from Kyev to Istanbul. We were required by the travel company to sit at dinner every evening of that Ukrainian cruise with a certain couple, with whom we found we had little in common He was a lecturer in dentistry and she his practice nurse. They were not interested in religion, but were avid film buffs. They described several films they had recently seen; in particular, one which began, it seemed, with sequences of unintelligible modern art. After a few minutes an usherette approached their seats and suggested they should use some glasses, and she handed a pair to each of them. "That's exactly it", I said, but I don't think they understood to what I was referring.

THE LENS

Seeing nature's slow evolving, tracing planets fast revolving,
Focused through the lens faith renders, shows them in their fuller splendours.

Gaining disbelief's suspension brings a spiritual dimension,
Gives confusion clear corrective, clarity and true perspective.

Shedding light on imprecision, faith adjusts believers' vision,
Tells with awe enchanting stories, opens eyes to heaven's glories.

Bread and wine, 'though consecrated, leave receivers still unsated,
'til communicants with lenses welcome Christ who comes and cleanses.

Human deeds of love and mercy show iconic'ly, conversely,
Presence of the Lord now risen, viewed when witnessed through faith's prism.

Come, Lord, end our indecision. Grant our souls that inner vision,
Thus to see your glories freely, find you in the poor and needy.

THE PACKAGE HOLIDAY

By 6, as sure as eggs are eggs,
you're woken when cicadas' legs
Begin their daily rhythmic din,
whichever Costa Del you're in!
By 7 you're scratching every bite
you've been inflicted in the night.
How did those little beggars get
inside your makeshift mozzie net?

It's 8. Your turn to use the loo.
Oh no! It's one of those! So you
Defer your chance to gain relief
'til swimming off the local reef.
It's 9. ....Can't wait! You place your feet
in little treads. There is no seat.
Then, hanging chimp-like from a pole,
you stare into a gaping hole.

At 10 the bay in easy reach
turns out to be a nudist beach.
They stare at you. You're in the wrong,
because you've kept your bathers on.
So off you go at 11 to try
an empty cove. You soon know why:-
Just as you start to swim a treat,
sea urchins pierce your flaming feet.

By noon the pain is so acute
you're even pleased to see the brute
Who comes to make you scream and shout

ONLY JUST

by digging all the needles out.
By 1 you know you can't achieve
a healthy tan before you leave;
And locals come to gawp and grin
and snigger at your pallid skin.

By 2 the lager-louts wake up
and start their day by throwing up.
They saunter yob-like to the beach
with several ghetto-blasters each.
By 3 the heat is so intense
that you decide to get thee hence.
Inhaling dense exhaust and fumes
you long to reach siesta rooms.

The timetables by 4 you suss.
You fight your way to board a bus;
But when the chance for nooky looms
the maids arrive to clean the rooms.
By 5, if you're at all like me,
you're dying for a cup of tea,-
With proper cups, not mini-sized,
and real milk, not sterilized!

By 6 you're reaching for the tin
of used-up anti-histamine.
Protection calls for jungle-gel;
but that you left at home as well.
You've craved all day a cooling breeze.
By 7 there's movement in the trees.
But when it comes and gathers pace,
thick clouds of dust engulf the place.

By 8 o'clock your body burns
so much, you're into taking turns
To cool you down before you dine
with 'after-sun' and calamine.
At 9 you search the menu through,

ONLY JUST

but when the food is brought to you
You've ordered just the kind of meat
you didn't want and never eat.

By 10 o'clock you are...... (Oh, no!)
....reminded where the sewers flow.
At 11 p.m. you get to bed
and dread the night that lies ahead.
The traffic's roar, the screech of brakes,
convince you brochures make mistakes.
You'll get no chance to close your eyes.
Those travel firms tell massive lies.

From 12 to 1 you're bound to hear
mosquitoes buzzing round your ear.
By 2 your stomach's feeling odd
from what you've eaten... Then, thank God,
The disco ends at 3 by law;
but cockerels start to crow at 4.
At 5 the young blaze home to rest.
From 6 o'clock you know the rest!

ONLY JUST

THE RESIDENTIAL HOME

The Home had mostly women, so imagine if you can
How animated they became on welcoming a man.
The men had mostly passed away or simply lost the plot,
So Meg was fascinated; so were Edith, Babs and Dot.

They hastily concluded that he looked a decent guy,
So all four introduced themselves and looked him in the eye.
Then Edith, noticing his accent, asks him where he's from.
"I come from Blackpool," he replied, "I worked along the prom."

"Well, what brings you to London?" Meg enquired with cheeks inflamed.
And do you know what he replied, completely unashamed? :-
"I'm not like other fellows who are proud of their careers;
I'm just released from prison after twenty-seven years."

"Good heavens!" stuttered Babs, amazed, "Whatever was the cause
Of such incarceration?" After quite a lengthy pause
He said, "I killed my wife!" The ladies gasped, especially when
Old Dot responded eagerly, "You must be single, then?"

ONLY JUST

My father, being a trained carpenter and pattern-maker, treasured his tools to such an extent that I was never encouraged or expected to touch them, apart from to pass them to him as he was working. He worked extremely hard and hoped that by studying I would have "an easier life". When he died on 11th October 1974 at the age of 72, I stepped inside his tool shed and simply stood and stared in amazement. I was being "watched".

THE REDUNDANT TOOL SHED

Spirit levels quivered, nerves they tried to hide.
Pincers grew attentive too. Pliers stood astride.
Planes awoke for shaving. Saws showed polished teeth.
Vices, benched, with jaws unclenched, Knives in every sheath.
Well-rehearsed for action, wedges in their sets;
Mallets planned percussion and drills their pirouettes.
Chisels by the dozen, sharp, with gleaming blade.
Bradawls stood, as soldiers should, upright on parade.
Files were rough and ready, brace with bits aflirt,
Two-foot rules and other tools loth to be inert,
Nails and screws contended, vying for their turn,
Not a care and unaware what they were to learn.

Each turned round bewildered, sensed perhaps a catch,
Shocked to see that it was me fumbling at the latch.

"Henceforth you're redundant," grievingly I said,
"Your platoon will split up soon. The carpenter is dead.
Could I but be your master, I'd join your fun and games.
But father led me from your shed. To me you're simply names."

ONLY JUST

I was in charge of a Secondary School which was very close to 'The Water Lanes'. These were narrow walkways, alongside of which flowed a shallow stream. It was there that mischief and unsavoury behaviour often occurred and many a truant or miscreant could be found.

THE WATER LANES IN THE SNOW

Dear Vrangue Douit Committee,
What your Secretary most disdains
Now has disappeared! So give a welcome
to the Water Lanes!
Metamorphosis has landed,
bursting cisterns, pipes and drains,
Halting traffic, jamming phones,
but welcome to the Water Lanes.
Motorists confined to walking,
vehicles with tyres in chains,
Leave your glassy streets and pavements!
Welcome to the Water Lanes!
Radios inform of cancelled fixtures,
functions; - None remains.
Clubs, Societies and Meetings,-
Welcome to the Water Lanes!
Leave your icy, draughty kitchens!
Leave your wintry window-panes!
Warm your hearts on transformations
welcome to the Water Lanes!
Gone the bags of glue that once held
crisps with nasty-flavoured names,
Fanta cans and Coca Cola.
Welcome to the Water Lanes!
Gone the disaffected youngsters
seeking solace from the pains
Deep inflicted by their problems.

ONLY JUST

Welcome to the Water Lanes!
Gone the truant's spite and malice;
gone the Kevins cursing Waynes;
Gone the bully, gone aggression.
Welcome to the Water Lanes!
Catch the stillness, hear the silence,
sniff the air before it rains!
Taste and touch the fresh creation!
Welcome to the Water Lane !
Unacclaimed, your Secretary
soon finds further human stains.
Come the soggy slush, they're very
welcome to the Water Lanes

To appreciate this poem one perhaps needs to be aware that between Guernsey and Jersey there exists a rather longstanding, friendly rivalry.

UNWELCOME BEDFELLOWS

Three climbers, - exhausted! - A Muslim, a Jew
And a Jerseyman, fogbound and lost,
Found a 'B & B' farmstead; but when they enquired,
"We're full up," came the farmer's riposte.

"I'm afraid," said the farmer, "there's only the barn;
And the animals sleep there as well!"
So the three had no choice; they lay down on the straw,
Disregarding the dirt and the smell.

ONLY JUST

But at two in the morning the Muslim got up
And he woke up the farmer and said:
"I just can't sleep in there; it's the smell of the goats.
Is there really no chance of a bed?"

"No, there's not," said the farmer; "the only place left
Is the box-room I use as a store.
You are welcome to that!" "Fine," the Muslim replied;
He accepted, and slept on the floor.

Then at three in the morning a knock on the door
Woke the farmer again; 'twas the Jew:
"There are pigs in the barn! I can't possibly sleep
With the pigs! What on earth can I do?"

"Look! I'm tired and it's late, and I'm longing for sleep!
There's a couch in the lounge over there!"
So the Jew, he apologised, went and stretched out
On the couch, with his feet in the air.

Then at four in the morning, another loud knock!
Who on earth could be wanting him now?
He was <u>cross</u>! But he smiled when he opened the door,
Because there stood a horse and a cow!

ONLY JUST

WHERE IS GOD ?

"Where, O where is God?" the smarting victim cries.
"Where is justice, equity and truth to counter lies?"
"Innocent ones suffer and the righteous often fail!
" Why is evil, mockingly, appearing to prevail?"

Counted with transgressors, Christ knows anguish, grief and pain,
Present now with the plaintiffs where injustice boasts of gain.
Now He feels and shares the griefs by human lives endured,
Grants to all his endless reign who suffer with their Lord.

Grant us vision, Lord, we pray, to focus on your Cross,
There to view the passion that deriders count as dross;
Sanctify our burdens by the sorrows that you bore, -
All for our salvation, that we each may love you more.

Earthly tenants schemed to nip the True Vine in its bud,
Crucified your only Son and shed his saving blood.
From your blighted vineyard now flow drops of purest wine.
Graft us to your vine-stock, Lord, to share your life divine.

13 LIMINAL LIMERICKS

9W

"If 9W's the answer," asked Lee,
"Can you guess what the question could be?"
"Of course," replied Kay:
"Herr Wagner, do say,
Does your surname begin with a V?"

2022-23 Prime Ministers

You may think that I'm making a fuss,
But some leaders are bad, some are wuss:
Boris Johnston, the chump
Replicates Donald Trump
With his lies, - even wuss than Liz Truss.

A Bequest

Walter said to his wife up in Crewe,
"I shall leave everything just to you
When I die." Then she cried
And through tears she replied,
"You mean devil! You already do!"

ONLY JUST

A Cardiff Ghost
A strange ghost in a graveyard in Splott
Was observed seven nights on the trot,
He seemed in a dither,
Roamed hither and thither,
So they think that he'd just lost the plot.

A holiday beauty in Marrakesh
At the Kenzi Club Agdal Medina
There's a beautiful girl called Catreona.
Her broad smile every day
Is like Cardigan Bay.
Wow, I'm telling you, You should have seen her!

A Kiss
"Oh no," said the beautiful Asian;
"This isn't the place or occasion.
You were welcome to supper,
But a kiss is no upper
Persuasion for lower invasion."

A long, sad journey
The funeral, then cremation.
To my great consternation
As tears were shed
My SatNav said
"You've reached your destination."

Shellfish Identity Crisis near Herm
A shrimp out at sea in the Russell
Had a random identity tussle;
Feeling frisky and hearty
At a prawn cocktail party
He succeeded in pulling a mussel.

ONLY JUST

A Site

When two shockable Specsavers guys
Went online, they were sprung a surprise.
All they did was type <***con
junctivitis.com***>
What they got was a site for sore eyes.

A Speaking Clock

When the clock in the hall chimes, it beckons,
For it's human and hungry, Claire reckons;
It's a grandfather finding
That he's hungry, needs winding,
And it's true, 'cos he goes back four seconds.

Accident-prone girl falls again

There's a girl with no dad, we've discovered,
Who is accident-prone, but well mothered.
Only last week she was seen
In an upholst'ry machine.
Now we hear that she's fully recovered.

Ageism

When we were in South Africa in 2007 travelling along the Garden Route we came across a bungy-jump over a ravine, where there was a notice indicating that old age pensioners could attempt the jump at a concessionary rate. I wondered if they were just hoping to get rid of us geriatrics one by one, so I wrote this Limerick:-

This brief bungy-jump notice was hatched
On a ledge where the young were dispatched :-
We would like to entice
Geriatrics, - Half Price!
Special Offer! - With no strings attached!

ONLY JUST

Some months later I adapted it, entered it in a Limerick competition in a national religious weekly newspaper competition. It won first prize, £50

This Church bungy-jump notice was hatched
On a ledge where the young were dispatched:-
We would like to entice
Happy-clappies, - Half Price!
Special Offer! – With no strings attached!

An ulterior motive
When sweet Susan was kissed by young Neville
She rejected him, called him a 'devil'.
She explained, "He's a novice
Who applies at head office
For a job at a much lower level."

Annecy's nonchalance
All the students just tended to stare.
So the teacher asked one who was there,
"What's the difference, young Agathy,
Between ignorance and apathy?"
She replied, "I don't know and don't care."

At the Marriage Preparation Class
The young Priest broached the subject of dating.
"So, is sex before marriage creating
A sin?" asked the bride.
He just brushed it aside, -
"Well so long as you don't keep us waiting."

Atheists
A.N. Wilson's words, as from above,
About atheists, fit like a glove:-
"They're like some strange refusenik,
"Who has no ear for music
And has never experienced love."

ONLY JUST

Aunty Bess

With her wardrobe, so old, and a mess,
and a really bad name, Aunty Bess
has now met Skipper Jim,
and by marrying him
she'll acquire a new name and a dress.

Awaiting the Fall

Old Joe and his wife well recall
How their teenage love life was a ball;
But with eighty years spent
If she gave up for Lent
He would seldom find out 'til the Fall!

Being an angel

The Nativity play saw Alicia
As an angel, whilst, dim with amnesia,
The virgin was Per,
Whose mum consoled her:
"Darling, being an angel is easier."

Betrayal

When Nurse Harris strayed more than she should
Her young husband said, "I understood,
I married this nurse
For better or worse,
But not that I had her for good."

Bio Fuel

Now that Bath's public transport is based
On a fuel that consumes human waste,
At the bus stop each day
People notice the way
Number 2's keep arriving in haste.

ONLY JUST

In order to boost his slender majority in the House of Commons David Cameron risked calling a snap General Election, promising that if the Tories were returned to power he would subsequently allow the nation a binding vote on leaving or remaining within the European Economic Community. He mistakenly believed that such a vote would support the idea of remaining within the E.E.C.

Brexit
David Cameron ought to be tossed
In the mire that his folly has cost.
To enhance his position
Against weak opposition
He just wagered the nation! AND LOST!

British Airways to alter terminology
In the Daily Telegraph on 14th October 2021 a letter appeared from a Captain Colin Cummings of Yelvertoft, Northamptonshire, who reminded us that a decision had been made that air passengers were no longer to be addressed by the term 'Ladies and Gentlemen'. He then suggested to readers that air crews might already not be treating them as such.

No more 'Ladies and Gentlemen', mate!
British Airways have stopped that of late.
With courtesy discarded
and genders disregarded
they'll address us as 'Self-loading Freight'.

Burns Night
For Burns Night the host, Jock McCoffell,
Composed a long ballad of waffle.
We have not ascertained
What the haggis contained,
But agree that the ballad was offal.

ONLY JUST

Call to the Check-in Desk
"Just how long is this flight?" asked a toff
On the phone to a girl with a cough.
"I've a wheeze in my head,
Just a minute," she said.
"Thanks a lot," said the toff and rang off.

After England's poor performance at the 2010 World Cup, Manager Capello's offer of assistance receives a rebuff.
Said Capello, when out and about,
To a woman all crippled with gout:
"Can you manage, my dear?"
She said *"You got us here*
In this shambles, so you get us out!"

Car-Park Crime
Parked multi-storey, devils
Smashed cars, including Neville's.
Such crime at night
Just can't be right
On many different levels.

Catholics in Heaven
"Here in heaven," St. Peter said, "Dear,
We have rooms for all sorts. Never fear!
But we whisper in gloom
Near this Catholic room,
For they think they're the only ones here!"

Church weddings during Covid 19
The Priest placed ridiculous bans
On weddings: "No holding of hands,
No kissing, no clinging,
No dancing, no singing!"
I wish he'd just read out the Banns

ONLY JUST

Churchill's Embarrassment

"Your flies are undone," said a guest
To Winston, improperly dressed.
He checked in a hurry:
"Dear Lady, don't worry,
Dead birds never fly from the nest."

Churchill's One-Up-Man-Ship

"You are drunk," a derisory prober
Chided Winston one war-time October.
"You are ugly," quipped he
To that fellow M.P.,
"But tomorrow **I'm** sure to be sober."

Churchill's response

"If I were your wife, - but don't think it -
I'd poison your tea," said Miss Blinkett.
Casting caution aside
Winston Churchill replied,
"If I were your husband, I'd drink it."

Cocaine Importation

This was the headline in Tottam
Spotted by Anthony Cottam:
Without any hint,
In thick, heavy print:
"Man found with crack in his bottom."

Conspiracy fails

Miser Bill and old Will said one day
Secret assets they'd just hide away.
They couldn't decide,
But now that Will's died,
Bill knows: 'Wills are a dead give-away'.

ONLY JUST

Covid 19

Entimologists researching in Nantes
Claimed that ants could pass on covid from plants
In winter, when wetter.
They should have known better!
For their antibodies mean that they can't.

Covid 19 Postal Arrangements in Wales, 2020

Of the postmen in Wales an assortment
Will be working from home in deportment.
It will probably fail,
For they'll read all our mail
And they'll phone if there's something important.

Dave Brewing

Narcissistic school-leaver, Dave Brewing,
Found a job fixing mirrors by gluing.
He was pleased as could be.
It was something, you see,
He could always just see himself doing.

Di's cynical view of marriage

A young tight-fisted Welshman, called Di, leant
On advice a misogynist guy sent:
"Before marriage one YEARNS
For one's lover, but learns
After marriage the Y becomes si-lent."

Doctor's Opinion

Said the Doctor, who talked like a boffin,
To a patient who couldn't stop coughin',
"It isn't the cough
That'll carry you off,
It's the coffin they'll carry you off in."

ONLY JUST

Doing Nothing
Unemployed Social Worker, Kurt Dimmischt,
Finds his job satisfaction diminished.
In the words of the Bard,
'Doing nothing is hard,
For you never know when you have finished.'

Dutch footwear's demise
Long ago the Dutch race jumped like frogs.
They could bound, leap and spring over bogs.
Their inflatable socks
Helped them bounce over rocks.
Very sadly they've now popped their clogs

E. Mauger
(This was written after countless letters appeared in the local 'Press' from the same untraceable author, repeating the same bigoted arguments on the same ill-informed topic, attacking the Church)

Since the thoughts of a boring old-stager
Get repeated so often, I'll wager
They're the Editor's views
Who is so short of news
That he uses the pseudonym 'Mauger'.

Easter Service
At the Easter Sunday Service Father Walter
Said he thought the worship order he would alter.
He decided on a whim:
"As we sing another hymn
Mrs. Jones will lay an egg upon the altar."

ONLY JUST

Effects of Horsemeat
Incandescent, a German called Klotz
Finds, when shopping at Tesco's, that lots
Of the mince that they sell
Contains horsemeat as well;
And the burgers just give him the trots.

Encyclopaedia Britannica
"All these twenty-four volumes can go
Now I'm married to Mavis," said Joe.
His Press advert pleaded,
"They're no longer needed
For there's nothing my wife doesn't know."

English Instruction Book Needed
When a linguist, quite tongue-tied, in bandages,
Couldn't open his packet of sandwiches,
"These instructions," he said,
"Simply cannot be read.
For I don't know this number of languages."

English Spelling
English teachers have a problem that is chronic.
Take the metal can that holds a gin and tonic:
It's metallic!   How absurd
That a 'type of metal' word,
Such as iron, doesn't follow. It's ironic!

English Student's Nightmare
The Judge, summing up, scolded Joyce
For using twelve commas, from choice;
"Despite your repentance,
Expect a long sentence,"
Said the Judge in a very loud voice.

Enhancing the Figure
At car-boot sales a woman called Pat
Sells a whole load of junk free of VAT.
What she earns she invests
In enlarging her breasts.
This arrangement she calls 'Tit for Tat'

Exam Paper Confusion
We 'A Level' students in Splott
Were stumped by the paper we got.
The question that threw you
Was when they asked, "Do you
Want multiple choices or not?"

Excess Luggage
At the Ryanair check-in Sue Gore
Cried, "We shouldn't be charged any more!
Mine is not overweight!
…..'must be Gavin, my mate!
….. 's got emotional baggage galore!"

Fancy-Dress
For the Geography fancy-dress, Cicely
Claims she's planning on dressing up prissily.
"I shall go there," she said,
"As an Isle in the Med."
But I told her she shouldn't be Sicily.

ONLY JUST

Fly-blown

Being born in 1902, my father was just too young for the First World War and joined the army in 1919. He was too old to be called up for the Second World War. Instead, he worked in the family chromium, copper, nickel- and silver-plating business in Gloucester, where certain parts for aircraft were plated. To ensure there was sufficient food for ourselves, relatives and neighbours, he built a pigsty in the back garden and kept pigs and chickens, whilst I kept rabbits. When occasionally a pig was despatched and butchered certain joints would be cured, coated in salt-peter and hung in the kitchen. In hot weather it grieved him greatly when he discovered regularly that flies had succeeded in invading the meat, and it never seemed possible to remove all the eggs the flies had laid without destroying yet more large chunks of each joint. It was whilst reflecting on my memory of his disappointment that I wrote this limerick.

When the butcher's smoked pork smelt like dung
And was covered in flies where it hung,
He was wrong to say, "Damn,
Flies are eating my ham."
They were casing the joint for their young.

For the Sick
After problems with the Verger at St. Vent's
Father John announced at Matins, looking tense,
"Near the door, sunk in a brick,
There's a bowl marked 'For the Sick';
That's intended in the monetary sense."

Horsemeat in Tesco's
Said an angry young guy, Dylan Deith,
"They've found horsemeat at Tesco's in Neath.
Just between you and me,
We had burgers for tea,
And I've still got the bit 'tween my teeth."

ONLY JUST

Hugh's Wife
Hugh, prior to his marriage in Thame,
Had no sex with his wife, - 'twas his claim.
"It's true, Joe," said Hugh,
"Well how about you?"
"I don't know," replied Joe, "what's her name?"

Idleness rewarded
When a lazy young skiver called Gwyn
Asked for cash from his own next of kin,
He was spurned with a shout:
"Sure!   I will help you out ---
Through the exit by which you came in."

Joe's wife's revenge
Lazy Joe and his wife lived in Hitchen,
Where she hated his incessant bitchin'.
Now he's dead she just stashes
In egg-timers his ashes;
So at least he's some use in the kitchen.

John in Bonn
As he entered a toilet in Bonn
After dark when the day-light had gone
John encountered a hitch;
It said. "Don't touch the switch!
With your movement the lights will come on."

ONLY JUST

Johnnie Craddock's T.V. appearance

Fanny Craddock was one of the very first TV cooks. Her husband often accompanied her on the show, and on one occasion was heard to utter this quip.

Though much older than most people's nannies,
Fanny cooked for our parents and grannies.
As he watched his wife cope
Johnnie muttered, "I hope
All your doughnut-rings turn out like Fanny's."

Katie's Dilemma
"Are these headlines in print stark and weighty
Meant for me ?" wondered young widow Katie:
'JUST TWO WHISKIES A DAY
RAISE THE RISK, SO THEY SAY,
OF FALLING FOR SOMEONE WHO'S 80.'

Lady Ga-Ga
Dressed in meat, Lady Ga-Ga asked why
No-one ever intended to try
To strip off the joints
And reveal certain points,
But it's just that the steaks were too high.

Lenten Confession
I've a flaw, and I should be eschewing it:
I procrastinate, constantly ruing it.
It was once my intent
To give up during Lent,
But I never quite got round to doing it.

ONLY JUST

Lettuce

An old Jerseyman felt rather queer,
As if lettuce was stuck up his rear.
The young doctor he saw
Took a look and said, "Cor,
It's the tip of the iceberg, I fear."

Lost Property

A sarcastic Headmaster in Goole
Held up underwear found in a pool.
He enquired of poor Sue
In Assembly, "Did you
Drop your knickers on YOUR way to school?"

Marriage benefits

In discussions on marriage, the Rangers
Said it often averts many dangers:-
"One should never disparage;
If it wasn't for marriage
Everyone would be fighting with strangers."

The cynical card-player's lament

"This is how every marriage is made,"
Said my card-playing friend, "I'm afraid
It's so good when it starts,
With one diamond, two hearts,
But it ends with a club and a spade."

Mathematical limerick

A dozen, a gross and a score,
Plus three times the square root of four,
Divided by seven,
Plus five times eleven,
Makes nine squared plus a little bit more.

Mental arithmetic

In his Maths lesson, measuring cables
On the floor worked a lad, Teddy Gables.
"Why the floor, little Ted?"
"Well, Sir, you just said
We should do it without using tables."

Michel de Montaigne's description of marriage

'Like a cage' best describes it, no doubt.
That's what marriage is mostly about.
Birds outside make a din
For they long to get in.
Those inside seem to want to get out.

Ed Miliband was made leader of the Labour Party, rather than his brother David, largely as a result of support from the Trade Unions. David moved to work in America.

Miliband

There are three with the name 'Miliband',
Two of whose aural sounds should be banned.
There is Ed, (and his mates),
And there's Dave (in the States),
So that just leaves the Glenn Miller Band.

Milk on Tap

When a breast-feeding mother in Mold
Was observed by her bright 4-year-old,
The child said, "Perhaps
Your breasts are like taps,
One's for hot milk, the other's for cold."

Mistaken Identity

A male hedgehog got into its head
That a hairbrush would make a nice bed.
It soon clambered off
Discharging a cough;
"We can all be mistaken," he said.

A Misunderstanding

Whilst on holiday Joan took exception
To a notice that caused misconception.
The hotel had a rule:-
"If in need of a stool
In the bathroom please contact reception."

Mr. Berlusconi

Though he wore Presidential regalia
Berlusconi was rated a failure.
The economy fell,
And while shares fell as well
He made hay with his Powergen Italia.

On retirement after 15 years as Headmaster of St Peter Port School in 1995 the Parent Teacher Association kindly presented me with a set of golf clubs.

My Golfing Career

"All your clubs are too long," said Joe Setter.
(He's my golf coach, who wrote me this letter.)
"If you cut off the end
You'll discover, my friend,
That they'll fit in the dustbin much better."

ONLY JUST

My Operation
My anesthetist's recommendation
Is for gas for my next operation,
"Or a paddle-boat blade,
Which would hurt, I'm afraid;
It's an either-or oar situation."

My useless torch
As I grope in the dark in my barge
My new torch is no use, 'tho it's large.
It's my fault, is it not,
For the batteries I've got
Were all given away free of charge?

"Name Change"
In November 2018 'Weight-watchers' announced that they were to be re-branded and would be known in the future as 'W – W' This limerick was emailed to the Daily Telegraph, who included it in their 'Letters Page' the next day.

The changing to 'W – W'
Of 'Weight-Watchers' name could well trouble you.
I'd prefer them to say
That they'll halve what I weigh.
You don't want to think that that they'll double you.

No B & Q
"In the Somerset village of Tarr
There's no B & Q there," shouted Pa.
"Of course not," cried Ann,
"You silly old man!
There's a T and an A double R."

ONLY JUST

Nurse's clumsy injection technique
Whilst asking donors' blood types, out of habit,
The blood donation nurse would tend to jab it.
But when a Priest and Imam came
in with a rabbit, "I'm to blame;
I'm probably a type-'O'," said the rabbit.

Olympic Athlete
With the athletes in national kits
An official asked one wearing mitts,
"Are you a pole-vaulter?"
He gasped without falter,
"No, I'm German and **my** name is Fritz."
(or) *"Nein, 'bin Deutscher, und **ich** heisse Fritz."*

Our Reputation
'May She Defend our Laws'
In September, 2020 Prime Minister Johnson decided to break the law by disregarding part of a Brexit agreement he had signed earlier in the year.

Our world standing's in cesspits and pools
For the Tories are acting like fools.
Though it's what the world craves,
And we once ruled the waves,
Boris Johnson keeps waving the rules.

Over-celebrating on retaining the Ashes at the Oval, 2013
Urinating on winning the cricket!
Whom to blame and on whom should they stick it?
One couldn't say which
Of them peed on the pitch.
All were caught on a damp, sticky wicket.

ONLY JUST

Overcharging

Overcharging was blatant deception,
So I said to the girl at Reception,
"Well, I never forget
People's faces, and yet
In your case I'll make an exception!"

Parade Ground Reprimand

"We didn't see you, Private Root,"
screamed Sergeant, (a brute by repute),
"this morning when raining
at camouflage training!"
"Sir, thank-you," replied the recruit.

Perusal

Three similar words needing care
Are 'examine', 'peruse' and 'compare'.
To examine means 'view',
To compare implies two,
But Peru's home to Paddington Bear.

PhDs

An Irish shibboleth that's heard around Kilkenny
Is the odd way a PhD's pronounced by many:
Is it Protestant P aitch
Or the Catholic P haitch ?
Which is right and what's the difference, if there's any?

Well, when the Protestants insist at graduation
That PhD's require an aitch pronunciation,
With a twinkle in their eye
All the Catholics reply
That a P haitch is a legitimate aspiration.

ONLY JUST

Philanderer, Sebastian Wood
A philand'rer, Sebastian Wood,
Asked his latest if she understood.
He'd woo her in verse
For better or worse,
But not that he'd have her for good.

Pointless Shopping Trip
When our butcher exclaimed , "You should point less",
I'm afraid that we ended up jointless.
For he said, "write a token;"
But my pencil was broken,
So in fact it was totally pointless

Break-in at the Police Station
The police said, "they must have been tall,
For those thugs scaled a fence and a wall."
Every room had been trashed,
Both the toilets were smashed,
And they'd nothing to go on at all.

Poor Prudence
When a sly rugby guy with a fly-kick
Jilted Prudence, who claimed she was psychic,
She watched game after game
Seeking someone to blame
But she never discovered his side-kick.

David Cameron had to cut short his 2011 Summer Holiday

Our Prime Minister, Dave, got a shock.
Gangs of looters were running amok.
Not to over-react,
He replied without tact:
"First of all we must simply take stock."

ONLY JUST

"Pro conned on beach"

An aspiring professional songstress
Was seen flirting whilst topless and thong-less.
So her tutor's advice
Was, "I know he seems nice,
........But your progress is hampered by congress."

Pub Sign

Your pub sign,   *'SEA   and   SAND',*
Has far more space than planned,
As you can see,
Between the sea
And and, and and and sand.

Punctuation helps

Illiterate Launcelot logs
His work and his leisure in blogs.
He eschews punctuation,
Thus, "*I find inspiration
In cooking my family and dogs*"!

Really?

Nurse Jones seldom said what she meant;
Last week she said, " 50%
of mothers were keen
in 2019
to breast-feed their babies in Kent."

Rev'd Speed

Rev'd Speed, whose dementia is growing,
Drives too quickly without even knowing,
But he claims, to be fair,
That he has to be there
Before he forgets where he's going."

ONLY JUST

Roads Closed
For ROAD CLOSED signs the Victor Ludorum
Goes to Guernsey, though drivers ignore 'em.
Traffic jams make one fraught,
And my guess is, they've bought
A job lot, and they've nowhere to store 'em.

Roddy's craving
When he first set his eyes on Nurse Spencely
Roddy craved her affections intensely.
"If I said," whispered Roddy,
'You've a beautiful body',
Which is true , would you hold it against me ?"

Single Mum
Single mum, Emily Drake,
Needing some cash for a break,
Advertised : "Wedding Dress –
Hundred Pounds, more or less-
Worn only once, by mistake."

Space probe
With a solar space probe well in sight
Several Irishmen planned for the flight.
They applied what they'd learnt:
So as not to get burnt
They decided to travel at night.

Speech Impediment
A discerning speech therapist, Pat,
Told a patient who tended to chat,
"Your tongue tends to freeze
On TH's and T's;
But you clearly can't say *more than that*."

Strange Tunes
In a graveyard at night, just supposing
You hear music played backwards imposing,
Don't get all in a tiz,
You can guess what it is:
Some composer is just decomposing.

Talking to himself
"When I talk to myself," said Bill Price,
"People mock me; it's not very nice.
But they don't have a clue.
There's a reason I do,
For I often need expert advice."

The Bishop of Crewe
As the boring old Bishop of Crewe
Went to preach all the microphones blew!
When the Bishop said, "Crike,
Something's wrong with this mike!"
Folk responded, "And also with you!"

ONLY JUST

The Choir Audition
For the Specsavers' Choir, Susan Drumming
Was rejected for constantly humming.
Though she'd no premonition,
As a trainee optician
It's surprising she'd not seen it coming.

But it wasn't her sight disappearing.
It's her audit'ry ducts needed clearing.
Thanks to Specsavers' model
An audition's a doddle.
Sue was given a glorious hearing.

So the problem was not with her vision.
It's her hearing that caused the decision.
But with Specsavers' skill
This soprano was still
Guaranteed a successful audition.

The Commonwealth Games in Delhi
Our friends have all flown off to Delhi
While we watch the Games on the Tele.
Though we hope they'll see glory,
I've a variant story:
They'll probably get Delhi Belly!

The Doctor's Visit
I was told by a Doctor in Fife
"I just don't like the look of your wife."
So when I caught his eye
I said "Neither do I,
But don't tell her. You'd pay with your life."

ONLY JUST

The shoe-recycling factory
The people the firm is employing
Recycling old shoes aren't enjoying
Their daily routine.
I know what they mean:
They say that it's just soul-destroying

The Farmers Union Shield
The Farmers Union shield
For GM crop Spring yield
A scarecrow won !
A job well done.
Outstanding in its field.

The Farmer's Wife
An old farmer, whose surname was Relph,
And who'd plucked pretty Claire from the shelf,
Said, " I can't for my life
Keep my hands off my wife."
So he sacked them and worked by himself.

The Flat Earth Society
There's one group that makes claims we should probe,
Whom we treat with the patience of Job:
The Flat Earth Society,
With no impropriety,
Say they've members all over the globe.

ONLY JUST

Apparently this incident happened when President Chirac, on an Official Visit to London, was sitting beside Her Majesty the Queen in the horse-drawn Royal Coach.

The French President's Official Visit
The Royal carriage carried Chirac. Well, of course!
But from a horse there issued wind with mighty force.
When the Queen said "Oh dear!"
He replied, "Never fear.
Don't be embarrassed; I assumed it was the horse."

The Hedonist Couple
An old hedonist couple from Crewe
Died intestate. They claimed that they knew
Making wills was implying,
That soon they'd be dying.
That's the last thing they wanted to do.

Ignorami
Foolish folk, what will always impress them,
But the wise, it will tend to depress them,
Is the fact that a lot
Of the people who've got
No ideas can always express them.

The Lady Cyclist
A delightful young lady in Bude
Often cycles to work in the nude.
You would think, from afar,
She was wearing a bra,
But in fact both her breasts are tattooed.

ONLY JUST

The Former Leader of the Labour Opposition
"With a name as if internet-planned,"
Say subscribers who don't understand,
"There are parts of UK
Disenfranchised today,
Where they simply can't get Miliband."

The Lost Pilot
A lost pilot, whilst flying a Boeing
Took Immodium without even knowing.
Then, to give him the jigs,
He took syrup of figs;
He couldn't tell if he was coming or going.

The Nun and the Abbot
A young nun asked, "On greeting the Abbot,
When I kiss his hand, do I just grab it?"
Sister Anne was explicit –
"Gently hold it and kiss it,
But you mustn't get into the habit."

The Old Husband
The husband of Joan Hunter-Dunn
Maintains love at 80's more fun.
His lumbago's no bar
For it's not very far
From their cottage at 71.

The Sark Astronomer
A dim teenager living in Sark,
Who just gazed into space for a lark,
Said, "The moon is more fun
And more use than the sun
For it lights up the sky when it's dark."

ONLY JUST

The screw-top fizzy drink
His fizzy drink, Phil Hewitt
Attempted to unscrew it;
I tried as well,
Oh, what the hell,
A monkey wrench might do it!

The School Play Producer's dilemma
In her play, for the husband, Miss Leaking
Chose young Tom for this role she was seeking.
But his dad, with a frown,
Said "Oh NO! Turn it down!
What YOU want is a part with some speaking."

The Three Wise Women
Whereas Wise Men were led by a sign
To present to the Infant Divine
The right gifts, as they thought,
Their three wives would have brought
A nice casserole, nappies and wine.

The Yarn of the Barn
At Eisteddfod a Welshman from Gwynnedd,
Quite deluded, had dreams he might win it.
He recited the yarn
Of the big empty barn.
But folk found there was just nothing in it!

Tongue-tied
An embarrassed young student in Poole
Who mislaid his Thesaurus at school
Said, "It seems so absurd;
But I can't find a word
To describe why I feel such a fool."

ONLY JUST

Truanting ornithologist, Mark Rault
There's a keen, young bird-spotter called Mark,
Who played truant and made for the park;
Though the fledglings had flown,
He explained on the phone
He was doing it just for a lark.

Though you won't find him often offending
It was Music he wasn't attending.
They had learnt in that time
Of Vaughan Williams's prime,
But it's Mark who had heard 'Lark Ascending'.

This excuse from Mark's mum, Mrs Rault,
School just took with a big pinch of salt:
"Mark is not one to skive;
He missed school because I've
Had a baby.   It wasn't his fault!"

A dose of Trump's own medicine
In 2020, with the first wave of the Covid-19 pandemic at its height, President Donald Trump explained his understanding that, since science had provided the means for killing germs, some kind of disinfectant ought easily to be made available that could eradicate this particular Corona virus from the human race. On September 30th, four weeks before the Presidential election which might give him a second term in office in the White House, he himself, having failed to heed warnings to take precautions and wear a mask, fell victim to the virus. Many a newspaper cartoon was swift to suggest he might now attempt to immunise himself with his own proposed vaccine, to protect him from becoming re-infected.

With a Covid cure well out of reach,
"I'd suggest disinfectant for each,
"And I'll show you," said Trump;
So, revealing his rump,
He injected his bottom with bleach.

ONLY JUST

Two classes of people
"In this world it appears what we've got
Are two groupings," said some silly clot;
"There are those people who
Would divide us in two
Different classes, and those who would not."

Unbeatable (for firmness, flavour and speed)
If we're hungry and desperate to eat
We just beat some eggs over the heat.
Putting scrambled aside,
They're much quicker if fried,
But a boiled egg you just cannot beat.

Undertakers
Undertakers who work on commission
Should be viewed with a little suspicion,
For they cannot survive
If their shares take a dive,
As **they're** dealing with stiff competition.

Verrucas
A young guy that I met on a cruise
Said verrucas had been in the news,
And some lads that he knows
Have got lots on their toes,
And he'd not like to be in their shoes.

Versatile French string player impresses fisherman boyfriend
This cellist's fav'rite dish
Fulfills her angler's wish;
With her sole, with *'grâce'*,
She will scale his bass,
And sometimes tuna fish.

ONLY JUST

Visitors' Map

"You are here," says the map on the pier,
With an arrow that makes it quite clear.
This amazed little Fred;
In confusion he said,
"How on earth do they know that I'm here?"

Weight-Watching

At furniture she loathes
Young Jane will utter oaths;
It's dark and tall,
But, worst of all,
Her wardrobes shrink her clothes.

What Door?

A knock at the door in Las Palmas
Awoke in the night certain farmers.
Someone opened the door
In pyjamas he wore.
Bad place for a door - in pyjamas!

Yet more horsemeat

Feeling hungry, old Ron went with Kay
To eat burgers at Tesco's one day.
When they asked Kay's dad, Ron,
If he'd like something on,
He said, "Sure. I'll have £5 each way."

Zookeeper's concern

He was not saying people were careless
When the zookeeper stated, in fairness,
That eating dried grapes
Wasn't good for the apes.
It was simply just raisin awareness.

ONLY JUST

Postscript

This outline of my life has been written, not because I regard my life as having been essentially anything worthy of note, but simply in the hope that one day it may possibly provide family descendants and close friends with answers to the kind of questions I wish I had been able to put to my parents, grandparents and their antecedents.

I have chosen 'Only Just' as its title because at times I have felt not only an admiration for, but also something of an affinity with one of my great heroes, namely the founder of Methodism, John Wesley, who as a child was rescued from an upstairs window of the Rectory at Epworth in Lincolnshire when it caught fire. For the rest of his life, he referred to himself as being, in more sense than one, 'A brand plucked from the burning'.

In a similar way, perhaps because of my survival as a sickly child and my subsequently being, throughout my life, very much underweight, I have wondered how and why I survived, for what purpose, and what I might ever be able to achieve. There was therefore something of a determination to try and prove myself, which some would call ambition, and a surprise at the varied, fascinating and demanding ways things turned out.

Many of the unexpected twists and turns of my student life, my subsequent career and my retirement, seemed to happen by very 'close shaves', 'narrow margins', 'only justs' and 'near misses'. Yet they took me through a love of sport, of foreign languages, of theological training, into service in the Church, into Public School as well as State School Education, and into twelve fascinating retirement years within the justice system of Guernsey's Royal Court. On the Jurats' Bench one's decisions had to be made on the basis of what was just and only just. Finally, being one of the longest serving Jurats, I was honoured to receive an invitation from Guernsey's Bailiff, Sir Geoffrey Rowland, to be sworn in by the Royal Court as a Lieutenant Bailiff, an invitation which I declined. It came just six weeks before my 75th birthday, when I would be required to retire in any case.

P.G.L.

July 15th, 2024

Printed in Great Britain
by Amazon